THE NEW
CAMP
COOKBOOK

THE NEW
CAMP
COOKBOOK

LINDA LY

PHOTOGRAPHY BY WILL TAYLOR

VOYAGEUR
PRESS

To our ray of light, Gemma Lumen.

In your first six months of life, you have followed us to eleven states and seven national parks, bounced along backcountry roads deep in the Rockies, weathered snowy hikes in Montana and rainy walks in Oregon, and slept on strange beds in tents and trailers and motel rooms. A born traveler and explorer, you did it all with such ease and big smiles, making friends wherever you went.

This book is just as much yours as it is ours, and the grandest of adventures is just beginning. Our greatest hope for you is a life of taking risks, dreaming big, and doing things that bring you joy, all while eating well.

We love you.

Brimming with creative inspiration, how-to projects, and useful information to enrich your everyday life, Quarto Knows is a favorite destination for those pursuing their interests and passions. Visit our site and dig deeper with our books into your area of interest: Quarto Creates, Quarto Cooks, Quarto Homes, Quarto Lives, Quarto Drives, Quarto Explores, Quarto Gifts, or Quarto Kids.

First published in 2017 by Voyageur Press, an imprint of The Quarto Group, 401 Second Avenue North, Suite 310, Minneapolis, MN 55401, USA.
T (612) 344-8100 F (612) 344-8692 www.QuartoKnows.com

Voyageur Press titles are also available at discount for retail, wholesale, promotional, and bulk purchase. For details, contact the Special Sales Manager by email at specialsales@quarto.com or by mail at The Quarto Group, Attn: Special Sales Manager, 401 Second Avenue North, Suite 310, Minneapolis, MN 55401, USA.

10 9 8

ISBN: 978-0-7603-5201-4

Library of Congress Cataloging-in-Publication Data
Names: Ly, Linda, 1980- author.
Title: The new camp cookbook / Linda Ly ; photography by Will Taylor.
Description: Minneapolis, MN : Quarto Publishing Group USA, Inc., [2017] |
   Includes bibliographical references and index.
Identifiers: LCCN 2016054283 | ISBN 9780760352014 (hc : alk. paper)
Subjects: LCSH: Outdoor cooking. | LCGFT: Cookbooks.
Classification: LCC TX823 .L89 2017 | DDC 641.5/78--dc23
LC record available at https://lccn.loc.gov/2016054283

Acquiring Editor: Thom O'Hearn
Project Managers: Caitlin Fultz and Alyssa Bluhm
Art Director: Brad Springer
Cover Designer: Amy Sly
Layout: Amy Sly

Printed in China

CONTENTS

CHAPTER 4
SMALL BITES

CHAPTER 5
CAMP FEASTS

CHAPTER 6
SIPS & SWEETS

INTRODUCTION

Picture this: It's a brisk and cloudless afternoon. After bagging a peak in the High Sierra, you hike back to camp and crack open some cold ones to celebrate another summit. Your friends come back with foraged firewood in their arms, and you season the steaks while they add logs to the fire pit. Hiking boots get swapped for sneakers, laughter echoes through the air. Salty snacks make their way around the group as stomachs start to grumble. An orange moon appears above the trees just as everyone settles into a chair around the fire. You watch the flames leap and snap as the first steak lands on the grill with a satisfying hiss.

Or imagine pulling up to the lake where you've been camping every summer since you were a kid. Now, you're bringing your own kids there. After delegating responsibilities of pitching the tent, setting the table, and gathering kindling for the fire, you prop your chair at the water's edge, sit back, and wait for trout to tug on the line. In the distance you see the kids setting up a slackline and the dog snoozing in the grass. Dragonflies skip across the lake to the soundtrack of songbirds in the trees. At twilight you're called back to camp, where a crackling fire and hungry family awaits your fresh catch of the day.

Whether hiking with friends or camping with family, I've found there's a lot to love about cooking at camp. The thrill of being in the wild can only be topped with a homemade meal, even when you're a hundred miles from home.

As soon as my favorite mountain passes and campsites open for the season, I start looking forward to my first meal in the woods. Over the years, I've come to find that cooking *in* the elements and *with* the elements (of earth, fire, wind, water, and metal—everything you need for an alfresco meal) is almost meditative.

Yes, cooking at camp takes longer than cooking at home. You have to start your stove or get the fire going, dialing the heat or piling the coals to just the right amount you need. You probably have to unpack a bit—and if you're like me, you go further, arranging your tools on the table and organizing any bins so they're within easy reach. Yet I see all this "work" as a good thing. Cooking outside forces you to slow down, take things in stride, and be more aware of where you are and what you're doing. After all, the weather and views will be as much a part of your meal as the ingredients.

There's also the indescribable: there's no arguing that there's something magical about cooking outside that makes food taste so much better. Maybe it's the woodsy perfume from a smoky grill or the sharpened appetites after an accomplished day of adventure. Maybe it's the simple fact that fresh ingredients don't need much in the way of preparation. Their flavors and textures are allowed to shine through in dishes that seldom demand a lot of effort to put together.

The first time I went camping with a large group of friends, I was getting away for my twenty-eighth birthday on a sweltering summer weekend. Eleven of us caravanned from Los Angeles to Kings Canyon, six hours away from the congestion of city life and into the primitive beauty of the national forest. We camped on the banks of the Kings River, rafted down Class III rapids, lounged in inner tubes, and cooled off in swimming holes.

What we remembered most, however, were the nights we spent sitting around the campfire, grilling meats and vegetables and passing bottles of wine and whiskey. With only the rise of the moon to guide our concept of time and no curfew of life to rush us along, dreams were shared while inhibitions were shed. Long and honest conversations mixed with laughter and lighthearted chatter until the last embers finally faded deep into the night.

Camping brought us outside, but the meals brought us together.

That river trip kicked off a big campout every summer that moved from place to place but stuck to three key principles: good food and great friends gathered around a roaring fire. No matter where we were headed—from Kern River to Sherwin Creek and from Florence Lake to Sequoia National Park—every camping trip began with a stop at a grocery store and cars loaded to the roof with enough food to feed us for a week (even if we were only camping for a couple of nights).

Food made every trip more fun—the collective preparation, the lively banter at the grill, the meals shared with friends under the glow of headlamps. The meals we made weren't just sustenance—they were a celebration of life outdoors, a nod to living slow and eating well.

Today's camping menus are no longer confined to the standard fare of franks and beans or "just add water" meals in a bag. They're fresher and healthier, if not a more simplified version of how and what you eat at home.

In this book you'll learn how easy it is for pancakes to come from your own pantry ingredients instead of from boxes. You'll see classic dishes like ratatouille take an interesting turn on the grill as colorful kebabs. Vietnamese bánh mì marries a classic taco in a savory culinary mashup. Shrimp and scallops simmer in a foil pouch of spices, sausages, potatoes, and corn to bring your favorite seafood boil into the woods without the big pot—or the big mess.

While some might be nostalgic, these are not the same recipes you remember from your Scout days, or from family road trips you took every summer as a child. They're inspired by real food and global flavors, and reflect advances in camp cuisine as well as a modern, healthful approach to cooking and eating outdoors. At the same time, they're still fun and unfussy. If your last memory of campfire cooking was a burnt hot dog on a cold bun, they may even rekindle your love of the live fire.

Away from home and under the open sky, cooking is stripped down to the bare essentials, so food becomes its own adventure—but don't mistake adventure to mean nerve-wracking or hard. Cooking in camp can be as easy or extravagant as you want it to be, but the experience in itself triggers all the senses, making you feel alive and free. There's a definite pleasure in escaping from our reliance on our kitchens, with their sleek appliances and specialized gadgets, and delving deep into our instincts—taming the flames and guiding the elements of nature to a delicious end.

Every time you make a meal or even a single recipe, it may very well turn out a little different than the last time. It could be the brand of charcoal or type of firewood you use, the salty air near the sea, the elevation of your campsite, or the fresh green scent of conifers blowing through the forest. And that's what keeps it so exciting.

Whether you're out for the day or gone on a weeklong road trip, whether you're traveling in a tricked-out trailer with a fully stocked kitchen or sleeping in a whisper-light tent with fire and foil as your primary mode of dinner, this book aims to equip you with the right tools and a repertoire of adaptable recipes for planning, packing, cooking, and eating well in the great outdoors.

RECIPE ICONS

Throughout the book, small icons above the recipes indicate the type of cooking technique involved in camp. Use them to help you find the right recipes for your particular camping and cooking style.

 Cooking on a Camp Stove
Stovetop recipes call for a skillet, saucepan, or stockpot, and some may require using two burners at the same time. If you're an experienced cook, you can adapt these recipes to cook on a grate over a fire with the proper cast-iron pans and pots (see **Mastering the Grill** on page 25 for tips on cast-iron cooking on a grill).

 Cooking on a Grill
Most of the grilling recipes involve a standard grate over a campfire, but some may specify a portable grill with a lid.

 Cooking in a Dutch Oven
All of the dutch oven recipes are tailored to cook directly on wood coals, hardwood lump charcoal, or charcoal briquettes.

 Cooking Over Coals
A recipe with this icon indicates food that needs to cook over a bed of glowing hot embers, so be sure to account for the time it takes to make coals from your fire.

 No-Cook Recipe
If you want speedy and simple, look for recipes that don't require any heat source.

SETTING UP A CAMP KITCHEN

You roll up to the campsite, throw the doors open, and tilt your head back to take in the fresh smell of pine. Your phone shows zero bars of reception. The distractions of home feel worlds away. As the dust settles from your arrival, bins and bags get dragged out of the car. A string of lights goes up in the trees. You pull a cold drink from the cooler, toss another to your sidekick, and start to settle in.

GATHERING YOUR GEAR

With the right gear, you can cook almost anything in camp that you can cook at home. While outdoor outfitters carry a slew of specialty items with multifunctional or ultra-lightweight features, the beauty is that if you're car camping, you likely already own most of what you need for equipping a camp kitchen. The only limitation is what you're willing (or able) to pack in the car and carry to the campsite. Start with what you have, and the more you camp, the more you'll figure out your needs for cooking alfresco.

Keep in mind that old pots and pans that you've outgrown can have a second life in camp. (In fact, my husband and I still use a set of cookware that was passed down through his family for over a hundred years!) Also, while modern cast iron comes with the convenience of being pre-seasoned, you can find buttery smooth nonstick on vintage cast iron. Scour your local thrift stores and flea markets to find pans with decades of use!

For some of my favorite sources, see the resources guide on page 218 or go to www.thenewcampcookbook.com.

ESSENTIAL EQUIPMENT FOR THIS BOOK

Every recipe in this book was created with and for the following cookware, so keep these sizes in mind when you're preparing meals or scaling ingredients.

12-inch skillet. Whether you're cooking for one or a family of four, there are few things this pan can't do.

2-quart saucepan. It's not just for making sauces—use it for boiling vegetables, cooking rice and oatmeal, or heating water for tea and coffee.

4-quart stockpot. Not too big and not too small, this pot can hold a family-size meal or a couple of bottles of mulled wine.

6-quart (12-inch) dutch oven. This is a good size to start with if you're new to dutch oven cooking. It's ideal for roasts, stews, breads, cobblers—even pizza.

Metal skewers. A set of 4 to 6 skewers, at least 14 inches long, can be used for toasting marshmallows as well as grilling meats.

Heavy-duty aluminum foil. A standard 12-inch roll is sufficient for most cooking needs in camp.

Cooler. If you frequently camp with a group, it's handy to have two coolers—a large one for food and a medium one for drinks, or one for raw meats and one for prepared foods. On longer trips, it may help to have a separate cooler just for ice, so you can refill your food cooler as needed.

Plastic storage bin. You'll need one large enough to contain all of your cooking gear, or a couple of bins to separate pots and pans from smaller items. Look for heavy-duty models that can take a beating in camp.

Camp stove and fuel. Car camping stoves are similar to your stove at home, and the best ones have powerful burners (upward of 30,000 BTU), auto-ignition, and wind resistance. For the most flexibility, choose a two-burner model that allows you to fit a skillet and a stockpot side by side. Most camp stoves are powered by small propane fuel canisters (sold separately), and you should pack at least two canisters, depending on the size of your group and the amount of cooking you plan to do. A good rule of thumb is to bring one more canister than you think you'll need.

Fire-starting supplies. If fires are allowed where you'll be camping, you'll need a few basic supplies for building (and extinguishing) a fire: a lighter or matches, a hatchet (if you'll be cutting kindling), and a bucket or other vessel for water (your dishwashing tub can double as a fire bucket). See **Building a Fire** on page 22 for more tips on fire safety.

Dishwashing equipment. You can set up a full dishwashing station with collapsible sinks or plastic tubs for soaking and rinsing, or you can keep it simple with a large bucket if it suits your needs. Add some biodegradable dish soap, a sponge and/or scrubber, a couple of kitchen towels for drying, and a scraper for cleaning cast iron. See **Dishwashing in the Wild** on page 37 for more tips.

General kitchen supplies. Never leave home without paper towels, hand sanitizer, heavy-duty drawstring trash bags, heavy-duty aluminum foil, binder clips (for closing chip bags and hanging damp dish rags on a line), and resealable plastic bags (the gallon size is the most useful for storing leftovers, marinades, and small pieces of trash while you're hiking).

FAVORITE KITCHEN HACK

No plastic wrap? No problem. Stash a few hotel shower caps in your gear bin—they're ideal for keeping flies off your food and covering bowls of leftovers.

Skillet. A 12-inch skillet is a workhorse in camp. You'll be using it every day, so choose a durable stainless steel or nonstick heavy-bottom pan with a tight-fitting lid for ease of cooking and cleaning. Some camping-specific models even come with folding handles to simplify storage. If you don't mind the weight, a well-seasoned cast-iron skillet is the only pan you'll ever need in camp, since it can be used on a stove as well as on a grill.

Cooking pots. For most cooking needs in camp, a 2-quart saucepan and a 4-quart stockpot will serve you well. Some saucepans come with pour spouts and measuring lines etched inside the pans, which make them useful as kettles if you're a tea and coffee drinker.

Dutch oven and accessories. If you plan to try some of the dutch oven recipes in this book, you'll need a cast-iron camp dutch oven—one with feet and a flanged lid. The 6-quart (12-inch) model is the most versatile size for everything from baked goods to soups and stews. Learn how to stock **Your Dutch Oven Arsenal** on page 33.

Dishware. Assemble a set of non-breakable plates, bowls, and mugs, along with flatware. If you grill a lot of steaks, a set of steak knives may prove valuable in camp.

Mixing bowls. It's good to have at least two large bowls that can handle pancake batter, salads, guacamole, and other group-friendly fixings. To minimize bulk, look for bowls that collapse or nest inside each other.

Cutting boards. It's handy to have two cutting boards so you can keep raw meats away from fresh produce. Go with something sturdy and large, and possibly one with a drip groove to help contain liquids from grilled steak or juicy tomatoes. If you're short on space, pack a few flexible cutting mats instead.

Knives. Pack a chef's knife, along with a paring knife or serrated knife, depending on your cooking needs. Wrap them in a thick dish towel secured with a rubber band to protect them in transit. If you don't want to bring your good knife from home, invest in one for camp that you won't worry about losing. Ceramic knives, in particular, are perfect for camping. They're sharp (and retain their sharpness far longer than traditional steel blades), ultra lightweight, and a good value, with most of them priced under $20. Many also come with sheaths to protect the blades.

FAVORITE KITCHEN HACK

If you like to make pancakes, omelets, baked goods, and other recipes that require whisking, a standalone whisk might be a worthy addition to your camping utensil set. But you can easily improvise a whisk in camp using two forks—place one on top of the other, with the tips of the tines touching, and whisk away.

Tools and utensils. At minimum, you should have a large sturdy spoon, spatula, tongs, scissors or kitchen shears, metal skewers, measuring cups and spoons, a cheese grater (which can double as a citrus zester), vegetable peeler (which can double as a cheese slicer), can opener, bottle opener, and wine opener. If you want to get grilling, find out what you need for **Your Grilling Toolbox** on page 27.

Headlamp. This hands-free lamp is handy in countless situations in camp, including cooking and dishwashing at night, and focuses light where you need it. (Be sure to bring extra batteries!)

GEAR THAT'S GOOD TO HAVE (BUT ISN'T ESSENTIAL)

If you like to be well prepared, these items are worth packing to make your camp cooking experience an easier one.

Camp coffee kit. Can't start the day without a shot of caffeine? Keep a coffee kit close at hand so you don't have to dig though your bins in the morning. See page 201 to learn how to make one.

Tablecloth. Picnic tables at campgrounds can sometimes be a little unsightly. Bring a durable tablecloth (at least 72 inches long) to cover stains, provide a clean surface for food preparation, and add ambience to your campsite. Keep clamps handy to secure the cloth to the table in case of wind.

Food storage containers. Find a small, lightweight, non-breakable set that nests. The containers are useful for packing lunches and leftovers, and can double as mixing bowls in a pinch.

Pot holder or ovenproof mitt. A simple silicone one can also function as a trivet.

Disposable gloves. They come in handy for picking up trash and working with raw meats.

Antibacterial wipes. At the end of a camping trip, these are super convenient for wiping down your stove, tables, and other gear.

First aid kit. Assuming you already carry first aid while camping, you can just pack a small kit with your kitchen gear that's specific to common cooking accidents, such as cuts and burns.

STOCKING YOUR PANTRY

A well-stocked pantry is a critical component of any camp kitchen. Pantry foods form the basis of all good recipes, and having the right items on hand can add great depth of flavor to a dish or make a meal more complete. Since you can't roll with a full spice rack or travel with all your favorite oils and vinegars from home, it's important to hone in on ingredients that provide maximum flavor for the most meals.

So, how do you decide what makes the cut? Make a list of the kinds of things you like to cook and eat in camp, which may be different from what you cook and eat at home. Stock your pantry with nonperishable staples from those recipes and stash it in a dry, cool place. A permanent pantry filled with frequently used items means you have one less thing to think about before a trip.

To organize your pantry, you'll need a **plastic storage bin** and a few **smaller bins or bags** to hold loose items together. Go with a heavy-duty bin, ideally one that can be padlocked to prevent rodents and critters from rummaging through your food. (You won't believe how quick and dexterous some of those animals can be!)

Just like your gear, your pantry will be specific to you, your cooking style, and your eating habits. While the suggestions on these pages are a good start for the novice (or infrequent) camp cook, they will certainly evolve with your palate and personal preferences.

Remember to sit down and reassess your pantry at the beginning and end of each camping season to keep it fresh and organized. Restock items that are frequently used, replace items that may have gone stale or rancid, and remove items that you've hardly touched.

Fats

As the building block of nearly every recipe in this book, fats are indispensable. After hundreds of camping trips, I've found that the few following are the ones I consistently reach for. As far as what I use the most, it's a can of olive oil spray. It's much more convenient than drizzling or brushing oil on your food, and it makes seasoning your cast iron a snap. If you like to use butter but always seem to lose it in the cooler, bring a jar of ghee (clarified butter) instead, which doesn't require refrigeration.

× Butter

× Olive oil spray (or your favorite nonstick cooking spray)

× Olive oil (or your favorite cooking and finishing oil)

× High-oleic sunflower oil (or your favorite neutral, high smoke point cooking oil)

Spices

Stocking a "spice cabinet" for camp is highly dependent on how you cook, but the basic spices below serve as a good starting point. Meat lovers may want to add an all-purpose steak or poultry seasoning to the mix, and if dessert is always on the menu (whether you eat it or drink it), ground cinnamon is a must. Buy small jars so they stay fresher longer, or transfer a portion of spices you already have at home to travel containers. Outdoor suppliers also sell miniature spice racks specifically for camping.

× Kosher salt

× Ground black pepper

× Red pepper flakes

× Garlic powder

× Dried Italian seasoning

× South-of-the-Border Seasoning (page 175)

Sweeteners

Granulated (white) sugar is the most versatile sweetener for cooking, but you can add raw sugar, brown sugar, or other favorite sugars as space allows. Buy the sugar sold in resealable plastic pouches for ease of storage, or transfer sugar from home to a travel container.

× Sugar

× Honey

× Maple syrup

Aromatics

Garlic and onion are my go-to ingredients for building flavor and depth into a dish. If you like to use a lot of garlic in your cooking, buying pre-peeled cloves of garlic can save a lot of prep time in camp.

× Garlic

× Onion and/or shallot

Condiments

While you don't have to carry the whole kitchen sink with you to camp, it's essential to stock a few kinds of condiments that can take a meal to the next level. You can transfer liquid condiments to reusable and refillable plastic squeeze bottles for ease of dispensing, as well as cutting down on weight and reducing breakables in camp. Inexpensive wine bags (the type with partitions) make great totes for organizing and carrying all your bottles.

× Vinegar (balsamic, wine, cider, or your favorite)

× Soy sauce or tamari

× Ketchup

× Mustard

× Mayonnaise

× Hot sauce or sriracha

Canned Goods

Though fresh is preferred over canned in most instances, there are a few staples I always stock in my pantry for sauces, soups, and salads. I like to buy broth in cartons with flip-top or twist-top closures for ease of storage in a cooler, and try to find quality canned tomatoes. If you can eat a tomato straight out of the can without making a face, then you've got a good one.

* Chicken or vegetable broth (or bouillon cubes, if short on space)

* Diced or crushed tomatoes

* Legumes (black beans, cannellini beans, chickpeas, or your favorite)

Quick-Cooking Sides

If you usually like to have some starch with your meals, all of these options cook in 20 minutes or less, saving you time and fuel. Tuck a small bag in your pantry and you'll be covered come lunch or dinnertime.

* Couscous (pearl or instant)

* Quinoa

* Bulgur

* White rice

* Pearled farro (farro perlato)

* Orzo

* Soba

Beverages

Keep all of your packets together in a resealable plastic bag and remember to replenish your supply every few camping trips. Coffee beans and ground coffee should be purchased right before a trip and anything left over should be used up at home rather than saved for the next trip.

* Tea bags

* Coffee beans, ground coffee, or instant coffee

* Homemade Hot Chocolate Mix (page 204, or your favorite hot cocoa/chocolate mix)

Bailout Foods

Maybe a rodent made itself at home in your grocery bag. Or maybe you returned to camp much later than you'd intended and you're too tired to cook. Whatever the case may be, it's always a good idea to have a few nonperishable bailout foods on hand for unexpected scenarios.

* Ramen

* Canned chili or soup

* Packets of miso soup

* Vacuum-sealed pouches of tuna

DROPPING THOSE FLAVOR BOMBS

Spices, sweeteners, and condiments aren't the only ways to flavor your food. By adding just a few well-chosen items to your camping pantry, you can punch up any dish that's lacking pizzazz.

Citrus zest brightens soups, stews, salads, and dressings with a tangy sharpness. If you're already bringing oranges, lemons, or limes, you can make them go the extra mile this way. A cheese grater makes easy work of zesting the peels.

Compound butters can make toast more interesting, but where they really shine is in garnishing grilled meats and vegetables. See pages 160 to 161 for a few of my favorite recipes.

Strong cheeses, such as Parmesan, feta, Gorgonzola, and goat cheese, can add a lot with just a little. In particular, hard cheeses (including aged Gouda and pecorino) can survive without refrigeration for several days and actually become richer in flavor.

Nuts impart not only flavor but also another layer of texture to a dish. Try adding pine nuts, pepitas, cashews, or macadamia nuts to your next soup or salad, pasta, fish, or grilled vegetable.

ORGANIZING YOUR FOOD

Having a calm and collected camping experience is all in how you organize, and this rings truest in the camp kitchen. Organizing your food and staying organized through your trip helps keep food fresher, prevents cross-contamination, saves money by cutting down on spoilage, and answers everybody's favorite question of "What's for dinner?"

From prepping ingredients to packing a cooler, investing a little effort in these seemingly trivial tasks can help you pull a meal together with ease and grace. (See **Food and Forest Safety** on page 36 for further guidelines on proper food handling.)

Planning Your Menu

In camp, the secret to eating well is planning well. While it's not necessary to follow a recipe for every meal, you should have an idea of what you want to eat each day so you can shop, prepare, and cook with less waste. By getting a game plan together before you even hit the road, you'll have done all the hard work already and can simply focus on the fun stuff: cooking, eating, and drinking outside!

Map out your meals. When thinking through the meals you'd like to make in camp, aim for a realistic mix of more elaborate recipes along with simple foods like cold sandwiches and grilled burgers. Plan to eat the most perishable foods, such as bread, seafood, unfrozen meats, and fresh berries, early in the trip, as frozen foods, packaged foods, and canned goods will keep longer.

Less is best. Try to include meals that use some of the same ingredients so there's less shopping to do and less food to bring home. Throughout the book, you'll find recipes with tips on how to "Use It Up," so you don't have to be stuck with, say, a partially used can of tomato paste. Plan for potential leftovers by incorporating them into the next meal (frittatas, hashes, salads, and soups are particularly good for this purpose).

Prep at home. Many recipes in the book have steps marked "At Home" that indicate sauces, marinades, and mixes that should be prepped in advance and brought to camp.

To further streamline your cooking, consider bringing a precooked meal from home for the first night's dinner that only needs to be reheated, or not heated at all (like a meze spread, page 11).

Timing is everything. Consider any activities you've planned during the day and make sure you've allowed enough time to cook around them—you don't want to come back from a hike at sunset, only to realize your dutch oven recipe needs three hours to cook.

CUT DOWN ON KITCHEN PREP

× Buy bagged prewashed salad greens. They save not only time but also water if your campground doesn't offer potable water.

× Pre-peeled garlic and pre-grated ginger in tubes (available at Japanese and other Asian markets) are practical shortcuts that don't sacrifice flavor.

× Slice and dice as much of your produce at home as possible and sort the ingredients into resealable plastic bags or containers by meal.

× Crack eggs into an airtight/watertight container and store in the cooler. They'll keep for 2 to 4 days and can be used for scrambles (page 59), frittatas (pages 65 and 85), dutch babies (page 217), and other eggy recipes.

Packing a Cooler

When it comes to coolers, the thicker the walls, the better insulated they are and the longer they keep things cold. High-end roto-molded coolers don't come cheap, but they're designed to hold ice for days and might be worth the investment if your camping trips tend to be long or remote. However, there are a few tricks for keeping any cooler colder.

First, start with a cool cooler. Since coolers are made to retain temperature, hot or cold, open yours up and air it out

Keep your food cold by packing cold food to begin with. Warm food or even room-temperature food will make ice melt more quickly. Make way for the entirety of your cooler contents in the fridge, and chill everything—water, beer, fruits, and vegetables included—ahead of time. Better yet, freeze them! Meats can be frozen in their marinade, and bottles of frozen premade sauces can serve as ice packs until they thaw. Nalgene bottles of frozen water are a feel-good bonus at the end of the trip when you've worked up a sweat from packing the car.

First in, last out. Pack the cooler contents in chronological order. Foods you'll be using on your last day should go in first, and foods you'll be using on the first day should go in last. Group ingredients by recipe to simplify meal prep and reduce the amount of time your cooler stays open. Put like with like—hummus and guacamole should go in one corner, while cheeses and other dairy should go in another.

Pack in layers. Start with ice on the bottom, followed by a layer of raw meats, poultry, and seafood (to prevent cross-contamination) and more ice on top. Assume that anything in the cooler will get wet, so store unsealed or unpackaged food in watertight containers and alternate layers of food and ice until the cooler is densely packed. Remember: Air is the enemy, and if there's still space left in the cooler but not enough ice to fill it, throw in the towel—literally. It will help push warm air out so cold air stays in.

Keep it in the shade while you're out enjoying the sun. If your cooler has to stay in the sun, try to cover it with a tarp or blanket to help it keep its cool.

Don't drain the water. Unless you're adding fresh ice, keep the water in the cooler. It's almost as cold as the ice itself and helps insulate the remaining ice. Preserve the chilly temperature by making sure the lid is securely closed and latched at all times.

Once you're home, thoroughly rinse and dry your cooler so that it's clean and odor-free for your next camping trip.

a day before your trip, especially if it's been sitting in a warm garage. You can even go so far as sacrificing a bag of ice and placing it in your cooler a few hours ahead of your trip. When it's time to pack, discard the ice and refill with fresh ice.

Speaking of which, don't skimp on the ice. When you purchase ice from the store, reach in the back of the freezer for bags that are super cold and solidly frozen. Even with crushed ice, you want big chunks of crushed ice, which will melt more slowly. Buy enough ice to fill your cooler to the brim, as any empty space will simply invite warm air in.

Divide and conquer. If possible, keep drinks and food (or raw meats) in separate coolers. By reducing the frequency in which the food cooler is opened throughout the day, you'll keep ice frozen longer.

BUILDING A FIRE

For many people, a good camping trip is all about a great campfire and the gathering of family, friends, and food that come with it. Many a story's been told and a marshmallow toasted over a roaring fire—traditions that are as beloved in backyards as they are in the backcountry.

Preparing food over actual logs is a time-honored tradition in camp, whether you're grilling (see page 25) or cooking in foil (see page 30). It's a deeply satisfying method that fills your entire campsite with the nostalgic perfume of "campfire smell" and infuses your food with a smoky, woodsy flavor. To build a campfire that burns for hours and makes great coals, you need three types of fuel: tinder, kindling, and firewood.

Tinder is any dry material that ignites easily with only a spark, such as dried grasses, dried leaves, or forest duff. It can also include materials you bring from home, such as newspaper or dryer lint.

Kindling consists of small sticks or twigs, usually less than 1 inch in diameter, that keep the flames going after the tinder burns out.

Firewood is any larger piece of wood that feeds the fire all night long.

There are several ways to build a fire, and even variations within them. Both methods that follow have their merits, so choose the one that is simplest for you to construct.

Teepee Method

Loosely pile a few handfuls of tinder in the center of the fire pit. Erect a teepee of kindling around the tinder, leaning the sticks against each other for support while allowing enough space between them for air to flow. Light the tinder inside the teepee. As the kindling catches fire, add larger pieces of wood on top. Start with smaller logs and gradually add thicker logs once you have good, strong flames.

TOOL TIPS

At minimum you need a long stick to move coals and logs around the fire pit, but having these tools handy can make quick work of certain tasks:

× A **hatchet** to make kindling from purchased firewood if you aren't able to collect kindling around the campsite

× A **small shovel** to clean out fire pits and move around coals

× A **bucket** (or dishwashing tub, see page 15) to fill with water and extinguish the fire

Log Cabin Method

In the center of the fire pit, place two logs parallel to each other with several inches of space between them. Lay a row of kindling perpendicular to the logs to form a base, and pile plenty of tinder on top. Turn 90 degrees, and lay two logs over the ends of the kindling. Turn 90 degrees again, and lay another row of kindling perpendicular to the logs. Continue adding more logs, changing direction with each layer, until the structure resembles a log cabin. Finish with two logs stacked in the middle for the flames to catch. Light the tinder and gradually add more wood as the fire gets going.

Preparing to Cook

Once the flames are low and the logs look like ashy chunks atop a glowing bed of embers (at least 45 minutes to 1 hour), you're ready to start cooking on a grill or directly on the coals. Keep a log or two burning in the back of the fire pit in case you need more fuel for the fire.

Putting Out Fires

Stop adding logs about an hour before you plan to sleep or leave your camp. Once the fire burns out, spread the coals and pour plenty of water on them. Stir the ashes, then pour more water over them until the coals have cooled completely. When you hover your hand a few inches above the coals, you should feel no hotspots.

MASTERING THE GRILL

Grilling embodies the absolute best things about camping: fire, food, and the open sky. It can transform ordinary food into meals that rival a fancy restaurant, and it has the unmatched ability to bring good folks from all walks of life together. (How many times have you seen people pull up a chair to the camp stove, clink mugs, sing, and strum guitar? Exactly.)

But that doesn't mean grilling comes naturally! If you're relying on wood or charcoal to fire up your grill, this section will guide you through the initial setup of selecting the right fuel and preparing for cooking. With a little practice, the meals you make in a fire pit or portable grill in camp can be just as gratifying—if not more so—as the meals made on a high-end gas grill at home.

The Lowdown on Fuel Types

When it comes to fuel for your fire, you have a choice of wood, hardwood lump charcoal, or charcoal briquettes, each of which has its benefits and drawbacks.

Wood is appealing to campers who want the old-fashioned experience of cooking over a crackling fire. It's easy to find

FIRE-CRAFTING ETHICS

✗ Always check with the campground host or ranger station to ensure fires are allowed, especially during periods of drought and high fire hazard. Restrictions are sometimes seasonal, so a site that allowed fires on your last trip may not allow them on this trip. Certain areas may also require a campfire permit.

✗ In campgrounds, build fires only in designated fire pits to keep your fire contained and lessen your impact on the environment.

✗ In undeveloped campsites, strive to build fires in existing fire pits if previous campers have left them behind. If you must build a new fire pit, keep it at least 10 to 20 feet from any tents, trees, or other flammable objects. Clear a circle about 3 feet in diameter, down to the dirt, and enclose it with a ring of large rocks. Be sure to fully dismantle the fire pit before you leave.

✗ Bring your own kindling and firewood if the park or recreation area doesn't allow you to gather fuel from the forest.

✗ Use only local firewood to avoid introducing pests to the forest. Some campgrounds may require that you purchase firewood onsite; be sure to call the campground or ranger station for more information.

✗ Never leave your campfire unattended, and make sure the flames are fully extinguished and the coals are cold when you depart your campsite.

and forage (if you're allowed to gather wood from the forest) and with a little know-how, you can get a fire going without resorting to lighter fluid. (See **Building a Fire** on page 22.) You can use almost any type of wood for your fire, as long as it is dry and not resinous. Hardwoods, like oak and maple, are denser and burn longer than softwoods, so they're most ideal for grilling. The downside to using wood as a fuel source is waiting for it to burn down into a glowing bed of coals in order to start cooking. But if you plan ahead, the woodsy flavor it adds to your food is worth the wait.

Hardwood lump charcoal looks like chunks of real wood because it *is* real wood—basically pieces of hardwood that have been charred into lumps of charcoal. Compared to charcoal briquettes, lumps contain no additives, light faster, and burn hotter and cleaner, so they're the go-to fuel for grilling purists who want a rich, wood-fired flavor. (Lump charcoal can burn up to 1400°F while a briquette fire might only reach 800°F.) However, they're also more expensive and burn more quickly. The heat they generate is less consistent, so they require a little more experience in managing a fire for optimum grilling. Depending on what you're cooking, this can be an advantage or a disadvantage.

Charcoal briquettes are inexpensive, reliable, and widely available in supermarkets and fuel stations. They're made from wood byproducts, binders, and fillers that are then compressed into their characteristic pillow shapes.

This standard size, form, and composition gives charcoal briquettes a more stable burn than lump charcoal, with a more consistent temperature over a longer period of time. For a beginner, briquettes are a good bet. However, they produce a heavy amount of ash, and instant-lighting briquettes, which are presoaked in lighter fluid, can impart an undesirable taste to food on the grill. Try to avoid instant-lighting briquettes altogether, or save them for dutch oven cooking where they're not in contact with your food. If you buy "natural" or "hardwood" charcoal briquettes, keep in mind that they take longer to light and burn almost as quickly as lump charcoal.

A mix of lump charcoal and charcoal briquettes can also be used for grilling to produce good flavor and consistent high heat.

YOUR GRILLING TOOLBOX

Having the right tools on hand will help you become a master of the grill. Here's what you need to gear up before you go.

Grill brush. A clean grill is a happy grill. Give yours the once-over with a stiff-bristled wire brush before every grilling session.

Chimney starter. Put down the lighter fluid and opt for a cleaner way to start your charcoal. It'll have you cooking in less than 20 minutes.

Stainless steel tongs. Get heavy-duty locking tongs with grippy handles that can turn heavy foil packs or hefty pieces of meat with ease. A 16-inch pair will safely keep your hands away from searing heat.

Stainless steel spatula. You'll need it for more than just flipping burgers. Look for a sturdy spatula with a low-profile beveled edge for sliding under delicate foods such as fish. A short-handled spatula is sufficient for portable grills, but you'll want a long-handled one for grilling over a fire pit.

Basting brush. An easy-to-clean silicone brush is useful for basting or glazing your foods on or off the grill.

Leather gloves. If you have to get your hands close to the coals, protect them with a pair of leather or suede welding gloves, which offer better heat resistance than silicone gloves or oven mitts.

Metal skewers. Forget those flimsy wooden sticks—metal skewers are far more practical. Get a set of 14-inch or longer skewers and you can kebab your way through any meal.

Preparing Wood Coals

If you're planning to grill over wood coals, follow the instructions in **Building a Fire** (see page 22) to get your fire going. Keep it on the small side, as it will cut down on the amount of time it takes to make usable coals. Allow 45 minutes to 1 hour for the logs to burn down into glowing red embers, then spread them out with a long stick (at least 3 inches thick) or small shovel to prepare for grilling. Once you're finished cooking, you can add more logs and make a larger fire for warmth.

Using a Chimney Starter

If you want an easy and efficient method for lighting any type of charcoal—without the need for lighter fluid—get a chimney starter for **Your Grilling Toolbox** (see page 27). This inexpensive and lightweight tool ignites charcoal cleanly, quickly, and evenly, and eliminates any hint of chemical smell (or worse, taste) in the food coming off your grill.

Place the chimney starter in your fire pit, on the charcoal grate of your grill, or on another safe, fireproof surface. Stuff some wadded-up newspaper in the bottom of the chimney, under the wire rack, and load it up with lumps or briquettes from the top. (Tip: Start more charcoal than you think you need, just in case you have to replace the ones that burn out too quickly.) Light the newspaper and the flames will ignite the bottom charcoal and channel heat through the rest of them. Once they get going, it takes 15 to 20 minutes for the charcoal to be fully lit. When the charcoal on top is mostly covered in gray ash, you're ready to start grilling. Simply tilt the chimney and pour the charcoal into your fire pit or grill.

If you want to start a second set of lumps or briquettes so you can replenish the first set as it burns out, leave a few lit pieces of charcoal in the chimney and fill it with unlit charcoal. This enables you to ignite a new batch without a lighter or newspaper, and without all the smoke of the first round.

Bringing Your Own Grill Rack

Many campsites have fire pits with built-in cooking grates that fold over the fire for grilling. If you're unsure whether one is provided, or you simply want a larger surface for grilling, you can bring your own grill rack or cooking grid. Grill racks designed for camping come with folding legs that enable them to stand over an open flame. They're useful when cooking for a crowd or camping in undeveloped sites, and for the serious camp cook, they make a worthy addition to a grilling toolbox. If you brought a cooking grid, you can create a makeshift grill by building a fire pit and balancing the grid between the rocks of your fire ring.

Creating Cooking Zones on a Grill

The secret to getting good grill marks while cooking your food evenly and keeping it from burning is creating a two-zone fire—that is, setting up separate areas for direct heat and indirect heat. With wood and charcoal fires, this is accomplished by banking the coals to one side of the grill. The closer the food is to the coals, the better it will brown and the faster it will cook. The side without coals will still be hot, but won't scorch the food cooked over it.

By varying the temperature on a grill, you can cook different types of food requiring different levels of heat at the same time. Use the hot side directly above the coals to sear a steak or get good grill marks, and use the other side to cook vegetables more slowly or finish a steak after searing it. The indirect heat side also serves as a flame-free zone so in the event of flare-ups, you can move the food over until the flames subside, then move it back to the direct heat side to finish cooking.

Cleaning the Grill

A little cleaning can go a long way, whether you're using the built-in grill at your campsite or the portable grill you brought to camp. Clean grates keep the remnants of last week's burnt-on grease from flavoring this week's meal and, most important, keep food from sticking to the grill. All you need is a grill brush, long-handled tongs, aluminum foil, and high-temperature cooking oil.

Start a hot fire under the cooking grate and preheat for about 10 minutes. The flames will loosen the blackened remnants, making it easier for you to scrape them off with your grill brush. Once the grate is free of food debris, ball up some foil and spray or drizzle it with a little oil. Grab the balled-up, oiled-up foil with your tongs and run it up and down the grate to coat with oil. (Safety tip: Never spray oil on a heated grate.)

Once you have a hot, clean grill ready, bring on the food!

THE MYTH OF THE POKE TEST

At some point in your grill game, you've probably heard about the poke test for determining the doneness of your steaks. It goes something like this: Hold your index finger to your thumb and poke the ball of your thumb with your other hand. That's what rare feels like. Hold your middle finger to your thumb and that's what medium feels like. Hold your ring finger to your thumb and that's what well-done feels like. But unless you're a professional, your poking finger probably isn't as fine-tuned as it should be.

To test for doneness, trust a meat thermometer: 120°F for rare, 140°F for medium, and 160°F for well-done.

Measuring Heat: The Hand Check

Without a cooking thermometer, the next best thing for measuring heat on a grill (or even a stovetop) is your hand. Place your hand about 3 inches above the cooking surface and count the number of seconds you can hold it there comfortably before you have to pull back. Since temperatures can fluctuate quite a bit with wood and charcoal fires, check a few spots for consistency before you start cooking.

High Heat (450°F to 500°F): 1 to 2 seconds

Medium-High Heat (400°F to 450°F): 2 to 4 seconds

Medium Heat (350°F to 400°F): 4 to 5 seconds

Cast-Iron Cooking on the Grill

If you don't want to carry a camp stove or simply prefer to use an open fire for all your cooking, cast-iron pans make that possible. They're burly enough to withstand the searing heat of a fire without scorching or warping, and they retain heat better than other materials. Char marks and burnt-on grease can be scraped off (or cleaned with steel wool for the really stubborn spots) without fear of ruining the pan—all that's needed is a new layer of seasoning to bring it back to life.

With a cast-iron pan, you can sear, sauté, and simmer on a grill the same way you would on a camp stove. Apply the same methods for preparing fuel and maintaining heat on a grill, place the pan on the cooking grate to preheat, and use your hand (see **Measuring Heat: The Hand Check**, left) to gauge the temperature of the pan before cooking.

In a Nutshell

If you take away only three things from this section, make it these three!

1. Always preheat your grill for about 10 minutes to allow heat to transfer to the cooking grate. A hot grill makes it less likely your food will stick.

2. Always clean the grill before you start cooking. Since you've already preheated the grill, cleaning it will be a snap.

3. Don't cook your food over a roaring fire. A steak engulfed in flames may look cool, but all you'll get is a sooty mess with meat that's over-charred but undercooked. You want low flames and glowing red coals for optimal grilling.

COOKING IN FOIL

If your favorite type of camping meal is one that doesn't involve doing dishes, cooking in foil—or hobo packs, as they're affectionately known—can be your greatest ally. This is cooking at its primal best: a handful of basic ingredients piled together, wrapped in foil, and heated over coals or a campfire. It's hard to mess up something so simple.

Foil packs essentially act as mini ovens to bake and steam your food. They're especially good for delicate, flaky fish and dishes that need to cook in their own sauce or juices.

Packets can be made ahead of time and stored in a cooler until ready to cook. Meals can be eaten right out of the foil, and leftovers can be wrapped up again for the next day. In fact, the minimalist camper can prep a whole weekend's worth of foil-pack meals at home and head into the wild with no pots and pans, not even plates. All that's needed is a fork and fire, and you'll be rewarded with a steamy, satisfying melding of flavors and textures.

Foil Pack 101

Always use heavy-duty aluminum foil. If your hobo pack is particularly heavy or full, it's a good idea to even double up on the heavy-duty foil. You don't want the foil to rip while it's cooking, causing food to fall out or ashes to fly in.

Oil it up. Spray a fine mist of olive oil on the side of the foil your food will be in contact with. It keeps the food from sticking and adds a subtle hint of flavor. You can also use coconut oil spray or rub on your favorite cooking oil.

Use the grill. Some people like to cook their foil packs on top of hot coals, but I prefer to grill them over a fire. It gets the meal going sooner, since I don't have to wait for the fire to die down to ashy coals before I can cook. Simply prepare a hot fire in the grill and wait for the flames to taper off a bit so as not to scorch the foil (and the food inside). If you already have a bed of glowing red coals that's at least 2 to 3 inches thick, feel free to place your foil packs directly on the embers (not in the fire itself). Cooking times will vary with how hot the coals are.

Rotate the foil packs. Use long-handled tongs to rotate the packs every few minutes for more even cooking. Keep an eye on the flames and try to maintain consistent heat, as with any type of grilling.

Be careful when opening. The foil pack will be full of hot steam!

Making Your Foil Packs

The secret to a well-steamed foil pack is making sure the pack is securely sealed. If any steam escapes, the meat and vegetables will burn or dry out before they're fully cooked.

1. Start with a large sheet of foil at least 14 to 16 inches long.

2. Place the food in the center of the sheet. Bring the longer sides up and fold the edges over to secure the packet, leaving a pocket of space to form a "tent" over the food.

3. Roll the shorter sides up to seal the packet, again leaving space inside for heat and steam to circulate.

MAKE IT AT HOME

Foil-pack recipes can easily be adapted to home cooking. Just prepare the ingredients as directed and bake the foil packs in a 450°F oven for the same amount of time specified in the recipe.

COOKING IN A DUTCH OVEN

Nothing evokes the romance of good old-fashioned camping more than cooking under the open sky and tending to a big, heavy, cast-iron pot the way the pioneers did. And while the technique hasn't changed, the tools that go along with it have improved dramatically, making the art of dutch oven cooking accessible to anyone.

Setting up for a dutch oven is not unlike setting up for a grill. You need a bed of glowing hot coals from a full chimney or a dying fire (see page 28) and a pair of long-handled tongs for moving the coals. For recipes that require more than 30 minutes of cooking time, have more coals ready so you can quickly replenish the heat source.

1. Light your chimney starter at least 15 to 20 minutes (or build your log fire at least 45 minutes to 1 hour) before you want to begin cooking. Prepare about 3 quarts' worth of coals and pile them to one side of your cooking surface. You can use a fire pit, fire pan, kettle grill, metal cooking table, or double layer of heavy-duty foil on dirt.

2. For searing, browning, boiling, or any cooking that requires highly concentrated heat, you want all heat coming from the bottom only. Arrange the coals in a full spread by spreading them evenly in a single layer, then place the dutch oven on top. The coals should be touching, but not piled on top of each other.

3. For baking, roasting, or stewing, you want heat coming from both the top and the bottom. Start by arranging a ring of coals just slightly smaller than the diameter of the dutch oven. You're essentially creating a burner for the bottom.

  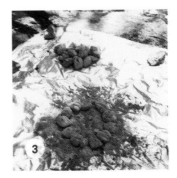 

4. Set the dutch oven on top of the "burner" and use tongs to place a ring of coals around the lip of the lid.

5. Arrange a second ring of coals inside the first ring, with every other coal missing, for baking on medium heat. This is the sweet spot for most dutch oven cooking, giving you an approximate temperature of 350°F to 375°F.

6. Periodically check your food by using a lid lifter to safely raise the lid so you can peek underneath it.

YOUR DUTCH OVEN ARSENAL

Modern accessories make dutch oven cooking cleaner and easier than ever before. If you're serious about cooking with cast iron, you'll want these items in your arsenal.

Dutch oven. If you're wondering where to start, a 6-quart (12-inch) dutch oven will meet most of your needs. Get an oven designed for camp cooking—it will have three feet on the bottom and a flanged lid for holding coals in place.

Lid lifter. It may seem like a silly extravagance, but this tough single-purpose tool is super handy for—you

guessed it—lifting a hot, heavy lid off the oven.

Chimney starter. If you prefer to cook with charcoal, a chimney starter is an easy way to light your coals—and light them fast—without lighter fluid.

Long-handled stainless steel tongs. A sturdy 16-inch pair of tongs with a good, grippy handle is a must for moving coals around as you cook.

Long-handled stainless steel spatula. Get a good strong one for stirring, serving, and scraping. The length keeps your hands safely away from the coals and a piping hot oven.

Leather gloves. Dutch oven cooking requires you to get close to the coals, and a pair of leather or suede welding gloves with a good-size gauntlet will insulate your hands and wrists from a hot lid, hot oven, and hot embers.

Whisk broom. An old-fashioned whisk broom is the best choice for sweeping coals and ash off the lid prior to serving. This is especially handy for keeping unwanted particles out of your food. Avoid plastic brooms, which can melt from the searing heat.

How to Cook without Counting Coals

Most Dutch oven manuals and recipes give you a specific number of charcoal briquettes to place underneath and on top of the oven. The basic formula for baking at 350°F is the "Rule of 3," which works for any size oven. Take the diameter of the dutch oven, subtract 3 briquettes underneath and add 3 briquettes on top. On a 12-inch oven, this equates to 9 briquettes underneath and 15 on top.

Another common formula for baking at 350°F is to use twice the number of briquettes as the diameter of the dutch oven, with one-third of them placed on the bottom. That means a 12-inch oven would use 24 total briquettes, with 8 underneath and 16 on top.

These longtime standards simplify the variable nature of dutch oven cooking because briquettes are generally the same size and shape. But different brands of charcoal give off different amounts of heat, and if you're using irregularly shaped lump charcoal or wood coals, you can't exactly use those numbers.

A better method for modern-day cooking is to use the "ring method" of temperature control—no counting necessary. In this book, I define temperature as 1, 1½, or 2 rings.

× **1 ring:** A circle of coals with all of the coals touching. The outside edge of the circle is lined up with the outside edge of the dutch oven, top or bottom.

× **1½ rings:** The same as the ring above with an additional ½ ring touching the first ring. A ½ ring is a circle of coals with every other coal taken out.

× **2 rings:** A full second ring of coals is placed just inside the first ring, with both rings touching.

The combination of rings for top and bottom heating correlates to the approximate baking temperature of the oven. I generally only use two temperatures when working with a dutch oven: high heat and medium heat. High heat (400°F to 425°F) is 1 ring underneath and 2 rings on top. Medium heat (350°F to 375°F) is 1 ring underneath and 1½ rings on top. (Notice that for baking, the number of rings on the bottom never changes. Coals are only concentrated in a full spread underneath the oven for searing, frying, browning, or boiling.)

This simple method works for any size coals. Since you need a greater number of small coals to make a ring but fewer large coals, the ring method produces more or less the same temperature whether you use wood or briquettes. With odd-shape and oversize coals, I break them apart with tongs to be roughly the same size.

While rings are a good place to start, their output can be affected by wind, outside air temperature, whether you're cooking in the sun or the shade, and how hot your coals are to begin with. Ultimately, you should let your eyes guide you by seeing how well your food is browning or simmering, and adding or removing coals as needed.

Maintaining Even Heat During Cooking

Since coals burn out at different rates and some may be hotter than others, it's helpful to rotate the dutch oven and/or lid 180 degrees every 20 minutes or so while your food is cooking. This is also a good time to check whether your coals need to be supplemented or replenished with freshly lit coals in order to maintain the proper temperature.

DUTCH OVEN DOCTRINE
If you can hear it, it's hot enough.
If you can smell it, it's close to being done.

Caring for Cast Iron

Start with well-seasoned cast iron. Most dutch ovens from modern manufacturers come pre-seasoned and ready to use, but it's a good idea to season them some more before you start cooking. Follow the instructions from the manufacturer on how to properly season your cast iron.

Avoid soaking your cast iron in water for prolonged periods of time, and never pour cold water into a hot oven to clean it.

Wipe the surface with a paper towel to remove as many food particles as possible. If further cleaning is needed, grab a stiff nylon brush, scrubby sponge, kosher salt, and/or plastic scraper.

Clean the dutch oven with a little soap. For stubborn spots, scatter kosher salt on the surface and work a nylon brush against the salt to loosen the grime. You can also use a plastic scraper, which makes cleanup a snap. If the residue still won't release, boil a little water in the dutch oven, wait for the food remnants to soften, and scrape with a brush or plastic scraper.

Wipe out most of the water with a paper towel, then heat the dutch oven on a campfire or stove for about 5 minutes until it's fully dry.

Oil the surface with a thin layer of cooking oil while the dutch oven is hot. Wipe excess oil with a paper towel and let cool.

Store the dutch oven in a dry, clean place, preferably in a carrying bag.

COOKING ON A CAMP STOVE

A camp stove is a necessity when camping. Whether it's boiling water for your morning coffee or stir-frying vegetables for a family dinner, a good camp stove lets you cook anything in camp that you typically cook at home. It's the fastest and simplest way to start any meal, because you don't have to light a chimney or build a fire. Just turn on the stove, dial up the heat, and you're good to go.

While camp stoves offer a narrow window of adjustability from low to high heat, wind and cold weather outside can greatly affect the output of the flame. A more accurate way to measure heat on a cooking surface—in the absence of a cooking thermometer—is with your hand. (See **Measuring Heat: The Hand Check** on page 29.)

Every recipe in this book gives a range of cooking times and temperatures, but due to variability in camp stoves, cookware, and outdoor conditions, it's ultimately best to rely on sensory cues (how the food looks, smells, and tastes) to determine when your food is fully cooked.

TIPS FOR COOKING AT HIGH ALTITUDES

Cooking in the mountains can come with challenges, even when you aren't baking. The low pressure at high altitude leads to lower boiling points and less heat output—meaning water will boil at a lower temperature and foods will take longer to cook. (This is why, for example, boiling water in Denver is never as hot as boiling water in Los Angeles.)

Since recipes are designed to cook at sea level, it can be difficult to figure out how to account for elevation when the present atmospheric conditions also play a part in how your food cooks. With that in mind, here are a few tips for tweaking recipes when you're camping above 3,000 feet.

× Pasta and rice take a little longer to cook at higher elevations. Add 15 to 20 percent more liquid and increase the cooking time by 1 minute for every 1,000 feet of elevation.

× The broth in soups and stews evaporates quicker during cooking, so add 25 percent more liquid than called for in the recipe and increase the cooking time by 2 minutes for every 1,000 feet of elevation.

× Because of lower humidity, watch for meats that might dry out on the grill. Move them to indirect heat (or brush on more sauce) to maintain moisture as needed.

× Baked goods are prone to being dry and crumbly, and as a result they go stale more quickly. Slightly increase the amount of liquid or egg in the recipe by 1 to 2 tablespoons at 3,000 feet, and add 1½ teaspoons for each additional 1,000 feet. Sometimes, simply using extra-large eggs can do the trick.

FOOD AND FOREST SAFETY

Being outside, basking in the sun, cooking in camp . . . all of it can make us feel giddy and carefree as much as it can make us care*less* with everyday risks we often don't think about at home. As with any outdoor situation, you can never be too prepared or cautious, especially if you're camping with a large group where small details may be overlooked. Brushing up on a few basics for handling food properly and keeping a clean campsite will make the experience more enjoyable for not only you and your group, but also other campers.

Handling and Preparing Food Safely

Since sanitation is limited in camp, it's important to maintain a scrupulously clean kitchen. No one wants to bring home food poisoning as a souvenir! Just because you're outside and being liberal with the "5-second rule" doesn't mean you can slack on your food safety routine. The safety precautions you take when cooking at home don't change when you're cooking in camp—they become even more important.

When it comes to food safety, these five key points should always be in the front of your mind:

× Keep your cooler at 40°F or below at all times. (Bring a fridge thermometer for peace of mind.)

× Never leave food out for a prolonged period of time. If food is sitting in the "danger zone" between 40°F and 140°F, it needs to be used within 2 hours (and discarded after that). Keep it in the cooler, warm it on the stove, or use other methods to keep cold foods cold and hot foods hot within that time frame.

× Cook all meats to proper internal temperatures.

× Avoid cross-contamination between raw meats and other foods.

× Always wash your hands before and after handling food.

Frequent hand washing is your best defense against foodborne illnesses. Always keep alcohol-based hand sanitizers accessible in the kitchen as well as in your tent and pack, or better yet, wash your hands (including under your fingernails) with soap and water. To simplify cleanup, heat a pot of water on the stove while you're prepping or eating so you'll have hot water handy when it's time to wash.

Camp kitchens often necessitate the need to reuse dishes and utensils when preparing meals, and while this is a smart method for streamlining your camp flow, it can spell trouble if surfaces are contaminated. Remember to wash all items that come in contact with raw meats, as well as allergens like peanuts if you're cooking for food-sensitive campmates.

Working with raw meats and seafood, in particular, require additional attention in camp. Without the luxury of a refrigerator and running water, the challenges of safely handling them are multiplied.

× Use a separate meat cooler if possible, or place raw meats in the bottom of a cooler to prevent their juices from dripping onto other food.

× Securely bag or double-bag all raw meats, or store them in watertight containers.

× Keep raw meats away from other food and use separate cutting boards and utensils when working with them.

× Discard used marinades immediately, or boil them for 10 minutes before using as a baste or glaze for your meats.

KEEP IT CLEAN

If you have to handle a lot of raw meats or seafood in camp, bring a pair of disposable gloves—it'll keep your hands odor-free and mess-free, and allow you to work more efficiently when water sources may be scarce.

Safe Storage Times for Chilled Foods

The following table lists safe storage times for perishables stored in a cooler at 40°F or below. See **Packing a Cooler** on page 20 for tips on helping your cooler keep its cool in camp.

Raw ground meat and ground poultry	1 to 2 days
Raw beef, veal, pork, and lamb	3 to 5 days
Raw chicken and turkey	1 to 2 days
Bacon	2 weeks (unopened package) 1 week (opened package)
Raw sausage (from meat or poultry)	1 to 2 days
Hard sausage (such as pepperoni or jerky)	3 weeks (opened package)
Hot dogs	2 weeks (unopened package) 1 week (opened package)
Egg, chicken, tuna, ham, and macaroni salads	3 to 5 days
Cooked meat, poultry, and fish	3 to 4 days
Soups and stews	3 to 4 days
Raw fish and shellfish	1 to 2 days
Eggs (raw, in shell)	3 to 5 weeks
Eggs (raw, out of shell)	2 to 4 days
Eggs (hard-boiled)	1 week
Liquid pasteurized eggs and egg substitutes	10 days (unopened) 3 days (opened)
Cooked egg dishes	3 to 4 days
Milk	1 week
Butter	2 weeks
Buttermilk, sour cream, and cream cheese	2 weeks

Safe Internal Temperatures for Cooked Meats

A meat thermometer is useful if you're uncertain when your food is fully cooked. Insert it into the thickest part of the flesh to test for the following USDA-recommended internal temperatures.

Beef, pork, lamb, and veal (roasts, steaks, and chops)	145°F and allow to rest for at least 3 minutes
Ground beef, pork, lamb, and veal	160°F
Hot dogs	165°F
Poultry breast meat and dark meat	165°F
Ground poultry	165°F

Dishwashing in the Wild

Dishwashing isn't the first task I typically leap at the chance to do (compared to the fun of, say, setting up the kitchen and accompanying bar), but give me pretty views, fresh mountain air, and dappled sun on the table, and doing dishes seems less of a chore in camp than it does at home.

A designated dishwashing station at your campsite makes cleanup a breeze, and uses less water and soap than washing in a sink with running water. Pack the following supplies in

your gear bin and you'll always be prepared when it's time to clear the table.

Washtubs. You need at least two large tubs for washing and rinsing. If you camp with a large group and do a lot of dishes, a third tub might come in handy. Plastic tubs that nest are perfect for this purpose, but collapsible tubs or sinks can be more convenient storage-wise.

Dish rack or mesh bag. You can certainly spread your dishes out on the table to dry, but a dish rack keeps everything tidier. Look for racks that fold, collapse, or nest neatly inside your washtubs. If you want to travel light, you can toss all your camping dishes in a mesh bag and hang it from a tree to air-dry.

Kitchen towel. Bring at least one towel for drying dishes, drying your hands, or a multitude of other kitchen tasks.

Scrubby sponge or dish brush. And if you cook with cast iron, a plastic scraper is useful for removing residue from your pan without removing the seasoning.

Biodegradable soap. Stick with a highly concentrated, environmentally friendly soap like Dr. Bronner's or Campsuds. A little goes a long way!

If you asked ten people how to clean dishes in camp, you'll get ten different answers. A lot of it depends on the size of your group and the amenities in your campground, but the following method has always worked for me in the widest variety of situations. Here's how it's done:

1. **Scrape.** Scrape any food scraps and uneaten food into a trash bag. Give greasy dishes a wipe with a paper towel. The goal is to get as few food remnants as possible in the washtub.

2. **Soak.** Fill the first washtub with warm water and a few squirts of soap and soak your dishes and utensils. The sooner you do this after a meal, the easier it will be to clean.

3. **Wash.** Squirt a little more soap on your sponge and get to work.

4. **Rinse.** Dunk the soapy dishes in the second tub of water to rinse.

5. **Dry.** Let the clean dishes drip dry.

6. **Repeat with pots and pans.** Once all the dishware is done, wash and rinse your cookware using the same method. If your pots and pans have a lot of grease or burnt-on bits, pour a little water in them and boil for a few minutes to soften the residue before you start scrubbing.

7. **Dispose of the dishwater.** Strain the dirty dishwater from the first tub with a fine sieve or mesh screen placed over the second tub. Toss the food particles in the trash. If the campground doesn't have a cleaning facility for gray water disposal, carry the gray water away from camp (at least 200 feet from any natural water sources) and fling it far and wide, preferably in a sunny spot so it evaporates quickly. Alternatively, you can dig a hole 6 to 8 inches deep for dumping all of your gray water so that food smells are contained to one area.

DISHWASHING DON'T

Never wash your dirty dishes at the communal spigots. Doing so leaves an unsightly and unsanitary mess of food scraps in the drain for fellow campers.

Food Waste Disposal

One of the cardinal rules of camping is to leave the campsite cleaner than you found it. Food waste, in particular, can spoil a beautiful setting as well as mar the overall experience of camping. You've seen it at some point: empty beer bottles in the fire pit, banana peels in the bushes, used napkins buried in leaf litter. Do your part as a responsible steward of our public lands by disposing of trash properly when you're camping.

If you're packing consumables from home, take them out of any unnecessary packaging to reduce bulk and cut down on trash. Repackage food in resealable plastic bags or containers that can be reused for other things. Buy beer in cans to lessen the chances of broken glass as well as lighten your load.

Try to cook only what you know you can eat. Avoiding leftovers—and the dilemma of what to do with them—is essential for maintaining a clean camp, reducing the likelihood of food contamination, and deterring animals from digging through your kitchen.

If you're unable to eat those last few bites off your plate, scrape the food into a trash bag so you don't dirty your wash water (see **Dishwashing in the Wild**, page 37) with excess food remnants.

Place all of your trash in a heavy-duty drawstring bag and hang it from a line or tree. Always keep your trash bag off the ground so it stays out of reach of critters. If the campground doesn't have onsite trash disposal, be sure to pack the trash out with you.

TIPS FOR CAMPING IN BEAR COUNTRY

✕ If you're not able to use a bear box or hang your food from a tree, a bear-proof cooler with a padlock can be a wise investment. Stash it at least 100 feet away (preferably 200 feet or more, and downwind) from your campsite when you leave for the day or turn in for the night.

✕ Avoid storing food, food containers, or other scented items (such as toothpaste and insect repellent) in your car and especially your tent. Store cosmetics and toiletries with your food when not in use.

✕ Never leave food unattended. It takes just a few minutes for not only bears, but also crows, chipmunks, mice, and other pests to raid your kitchen and daypacks when you least expect them.

✕ Do not cook next to your tent or leave dirty dishes in camp.

✕ Keep the clothes you sleep in free of food and cooking smells.

✕ In isolated areas, leaving a bright light on at night can help deter bears from rummaging through your campsite (but is not a substitute for proper storage and cleanup procedures).

✕ Food waste should be treated the same as food. If bear-resistant trash cans aren't available in the campground, trash should be stored in a bear box, hung from a tree, or stashed in a secure container and moved at least 100 feet downwind from camp. Avoid leaving trash bags loose in camp overnight, as you may find yourself waking up to a large mess all over the ground!

✕ Camping and cooking in grizzly territory requires extra caution. Always check with local rangers about wildlife activity in the areas you visit.

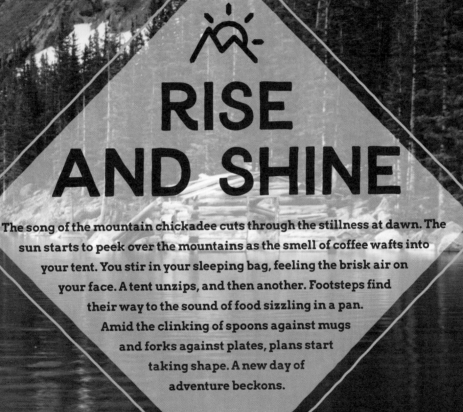

RISE AND SHINE

The song of the mountain chickadee cuts through the stillness at dawn. The sun starts to peek over the mountains as the smell of coffee wafts into your tent. You stir in your sleeping bag, feeling the brisk air on your face. A tent unzips, and then another. Footsteps find their way to the sound of food sizzling in a pan. Amid the clinking of spoons against mugs and forks against plates, plans start taking shape. A new day of adventure beckons.

Fresh, warm, homemade pastries at camp? Yes, please! Skillet scones are a campside take on Irish soda farls, the traditional quick-cooking breads made the old-fashioned way on a griddle. They're crisp and dry on the outside but soft and dense in the center, and are delicious with a smear of jam or butter served alongside coffee or tea. To make a savory version of these skillet scones, just swap the sugar, lemon zest, and blueberries for shredded Cheddar and chopped scallions.

BLUEBERRY SKILLET SCONES WITH LEMON GLAZE

MAKES 14 SCONES

FOR THE SCONES

2 cups (240 g) Multipurpose Baking Mix (page 44)

¾ cup (180 ml) buttermilk

¼ cup (56 g) butter, melted and cooled, plus more for greasing

3 tablespoons granulated sugar

1 large egg

Zest of 1 large lemon

1 cup (170 g) blueberries

FOR THE GLAZE

½ cup (57 g) powdered sugar

1 tablespoon lemon juice

To make the scones, in a large bowl, stir together the baking mix, buttermilk, butter, granulated sugar, egg, and lemon zest with a large sturdy spoon until a soft, sticky, and shaggy dough forms. Gently fold in the blueberries.

Grease a large skillet with butter and heat it over medium-low heat. Using a large spoon, drop ¼-cupfuls of dough (slightly larger than a golf ball) into the skillet. Arrange them so that the sides of each biscuit are barely touching. You should have 14 scones.

Cover and cook until the scones are golden brown on the bottom, 4 to 5 minutes. Turn each biscuit over with a spoon and continue cooking, covered, for about 5 minutes more until both sides are lightly browned and the scones are fully cooked in the center.

Meanwhile, to make the glaze, whisk together the powdered sugar and lemon juice in a small bowl until well blended. Drizzle the glaze over the warm scones before serving.

✧ USE IT UP ✧

Want to find a recipe for that buttermilk left in the carton? Use it up in Buttermilk Pancakes with Maple, Mascarpone, and Berries (page 52) or Dutch Oven–Baked Buttermilk Chicken with Kale and Apple Slaw (page 182).

Freshly made baked goods—that don't come out of a box or can—feel like such a luxury in camp, even though their core ingredients couldn't be simpler. But hauling bags of flour, sugar, and leaveners isn't really feasible, nor is all the exact measuring you have to do every time for every recipe. If you bring a large batch of this highly versatile baking mix, however, you can whip up homemade cobblers (page 215), scones (page 42), pancakes (pages 51 and 52), biscuits, coffee cakes, and other quick breads with ease. It also works in other recipes that call for commercial all-purpose baking mixes. Double or triple the recipe according to your needs.

MULTIPURPOSE BAKING MIX

MAKES 3 CUPS (360 G)

3 cups (360 g) all-purpose flour
1 tablespoon sugar
1 tablespoon baking powder
1 teaspoon baking soda
1 teaspoon kosher salt

Combine all of the ingredients in a medium bowl. Transfer to a resealable plastic bag or lidded container and store in a dry, cool place for up to 8 months. Before using, stir the mix around to evenly distribute the ingredients.

Note: I use the "scoop and sweep" method for measuring flour: simply scoop a heaping cupful of flour, then level it with a straightedge. If your flour has been sitting in the bottom of a bag or canister for a while, fluff it up with a fork before scooping.

If you like to start the day with a hot mug of chai, you're sure to love this bowl of chai-spiced oatmeal. A few spoonfuls of chai concentrate turn ordinary oatmeal into a rich and creamy breakfast that's as cozy and comforting as the tea itself. Apples and walnuts are a classic combination for sweetness and crunch, but you can also try pears, bananas, pepitas, or pecans. If you don't want to dirty another pan, nix the fresh fruit altogether and stir in a handful of raisins and dates. (Pictured next page, left.)

CHAI-SPICED OATMEAL WITH CINNAMON APPLES

MAKES 4 SERVINGS

3 cups (700 ml) water

2 cups (225 g) Toasted Instant Oatmeal (page 48)

6 tablespoons Chai Concentrate (page 202)

2 tablespoons butter

2 medium apples, cored and thinly sliced

⅛ teaspoon ground cinnamon

Chopped walnuts

Bring the water to a boil in a small saucepan and add the oats. Reduce the heat and simmer for about 5 minutes, stirring occasionally, until the oats are cooked to your preferred consistency. Stir in the chai concentrate and heat just enough to keep warm.

Meanwhile, melt the butter in a large skillet over medium heat. Add the apples and cinnamon and cook until tender, about 5 minutes, stirring occasionally.

Divide the oatmeal and apples among 4 bowls and top each with a handful of walnuts before serving.

In this savory spin on oatmeal, the grains give ricelike texture to a hearty, Asian-inspired breakfast bowl that can hold its own at other times of day. Using chicken broth in place of water amps up the umami factor—and you can try this trick for concocting your own savory oatmeal. If you have leftover cooked chicken from the night before, toss that into the pan too. (Pictured right.)

SAVORY OATMEAL WITH SHIITAKE AND SPINACH

MAKES 4 SERVINGS

2 tablespoons olive oil, divided

1 medium shallot, finely chopped

3 cups (700 ml) chicken broth

2 cups (225 g) Toasted Instant Oatmeal (page 48), no added sugar or cinnamon

8 medium shiitake mushrooms, sliced (about 3 ounces)

¼ teaspoon kosher salt

⅛ teaspoon ground black pepper

3 cups (100 g) packed baby spinach

2 tablespoons ponzu sauce, plus more for serving

Note: Ponzu sauce is a Japanese citrus-based soy sauce found in the ethnic aisle of most well-stocked supermarkets.

Drizzle 1 tablespoon of the oil in a small saucepan over medium-high heat. Add the shallots and cook until they start to turn translucent, about 2 minutes. Add the broth and oatmeal and bring to a boil. Reduce the heat and simmer for about 5 minutes, stirring occasionally, until the oats are cooked to your preferred consistency. Continue to heat just enough to keep warm.

Meanwhile, set a large skillet over medium-high heat and swirl in the remaining 1 tablespoon oil. Add the mushrooms, salt, and pepper. Cook until the mushrooms are soft, 3 to 5 minutes, stirring occasionally. Add the spinach and ponzu, stir to combine, and cook until the spinach is just wilted, about 2 minutes.

Divide the oatmeal, mushrooms, and spinach among 4 bowls and drizzle with a little ponzu before serving.

Many people have fond memories of starting their morning in camp by firing up the stove and tearing open a little packet of instant oatmeal. But you can actually make your own instant oatmeal quite easily with less cost and more control over quality and flavor. Start with rolled oats (also called old-fashioned oats), put them through a couple of extra steps, and they suddenly get more interesting. Here, a light toast in the oven imparts a nutty flavor to the oats, while whizzing half of them in a food processor gives the cooked oatmeal a creamier texture than rolled oats alone.

TOASTED INSTANT OATMEAL

MAKES 4 CUPS (450 G)

4 cups (400 g) rolled oats

¼ cup (50 g) packed brown sugar (optional, see Note)

1 teaspoon kosher salt

½ teaspoon ground cinnamon (optional, see Note)

Note: If your preference is for savory oatmeal (like Savory Oatmeal with Bacon, Cheddar, and Fried Egg, opposite page) or you like to control the amount of sweetness in each serving, leave out the brown sugar and cinnamon. Conversely, you can also add more sugar if you typically like your oatmeal sweeter.

Preheat the oven to 350°F.

Spread the oats on a rimmed baking sheet and bake for 10 to 15 minutes, stirring halfway through, until lightly toasted but not browned. Let cool.

Put half the toasted oats in a food processor and pulse until finely crumbled. Combine all the oats in a large bowl and stir in the sugar, salt, and cinnamon.

Transfer to a resealable plastic bag or lidded container and store in a dry, cool place for up to 1 year. (Alternatively, you can divide the oatmeal into ½-cup [57-g] portions and store them individually to make your own instant oatmeal packets.)

 ✧ **MIX IT UP** ✧

If you're making your own instant oatmeal packets, mix in your favorite flavorings ahead of time and all that's needed when you're ready to cook is a pot of boiling water. Try any combination of dried fruits (dates, apricots, cranberries), freeze-dried fruits (strawberries, blueberries, apples), seeds (chia, flax, hemp), and other add-ins (coconut flakes, candied ginger, powdered milk). I like to keep nuts separate, added only when the oatmeal is done so they retain their crunch.

If sweet oatmeal has never been your thing, savory oatmeal may just change your mind about the classic breakfast bowl. Let the traditionalists top their oatmeal with fruits, nuts, and milk; the rebel in you knows that bacon makes everything better. Cheddar adds even more punch to every bite, and an egg—fried in bacon grease, of course—fuels you up for the day's big hike (or big hammock fest, if that's more your speed).

SAVORY OATMEAL WITH BACON, CHEDDAR, AND FRIED EGG

MAKES 4 SERVINGS

1 tablespoon olive oil

1 small yellow onion, finely chopped

3 cups (700 g) water

2 cups (225 g) Toasted Instant Oatmeal (page 48), with no added sugar or cinnamon

1 cup (113 g) grated sharp Cheddar cheese

8 strips bacon

4 large eggs

Kosher salt and ground black pepper

Set a small saucepan over medium-high heat and swirl in the oil. Add the onion and cook until it starts to turn translucent, 2 to 3 minutes. Add the water and oatmeal and bring to a boil. Reduce the heat, cover, and simmer for about 5 minutes, stirring occasionally, until the oats are cooked to your preferred consistency. Stir in the cheese and heat just enough to keep warm.

Meanwhile, set a large skillet over high heat. Working in two batches, add the bacon and fry until crisp, about 5 minutes, turning once. Transfer to a paper-towel–lined plate and crumble the bacon. Discard the bacon grease, reserving 1 tablespoon in the skillet.

Reheat the skillet over medium heat. Add the eggs to the skillet one at a time, being careful to keep the whites from overlapping too much. Cook undisturbed until the whites turn opaque, about 1 minute. Reduce the heat slightly, cover, and cook for about 4 minutes, or until the whites are completely set but the yolks are still soft. (For medium yolks, cook for 5 minutes; for hard yolks, cook for 6 minutes.)

Divide the oatmeal, bacon, and fried eggs among 4 bowls and season with salt and pepper to taste.

Who says pancakes have to be sweet? Savory stacks are a surprising offering among the usual sweet treats of breakfast foods, and they seamlessly move into breakfast-for-dinner territory too. It all starts with my baking mix and the rest is up to your imagination. Swap the mushrooms for sun-dried tomatoes or forgo the goat cheese and melt Cheddar into the batter for oozy goodness. If breakfast is a big, fun, and boisterous tradition at your campsite, you can even host a "pancake bar" and offer a variety of add-ins (both sweet and savory) so friends can fill and flip their own.

FOR THE FILLING

4 medium cremini mushrooms, finely chopped

4 scallions, finely chopped

2 tablespoons olive oil

1 tablespoon chopped fresh thyme

½ teaspoon kosher salt

¼ teaspoon ground black pepper

FOR THE PANCAKES

2 cups (240 g) Multipurpose Baking Mix (page 44)

1½ cups (350 ml) milk

2 large eggs

Butter

Goat cheese

 USE IT UP

Where else can you use thyme if you have to buy a whole bunch of it? Put it in Spiced and Herbed Mixed Nuts (page 109), Grilled Watermelon with Gorgonzola and Pistachio Crumbles (page 133), Bacon-Wrapped Trout Stuffed with Herbs (page 103), Garlic-Herb Butter (page 161), or the herb-whipped goat cheese in Pile of Grilled Market Vegetables with Herbed Toasts (page 79).

SAVORY PANCAKES WITH SCALLIONS, MUSHROOMS, AND GOAT CHEESE

MAKES 4 SERVINGS

To make the filling, in a small bowl, combine the mushrooms, scallions, oil, thyme, salt, and pepper and set aside.

To make the pancakes, in a large bowl, whisk the baking mix with the milk and eggs until well blended.

Heat a large skillet over medium heat and melt a pat of butter, swirling to coat the surface. Ladle ¼ cup (60 ml) batter at a time into the skillet. Sprinkle 2 heaping tablespoons of the mushroom and scallion mixture over the batter and lightly press it into the pancake as it cooks. Cook until the edges begin to set, about 3 minutes. Flip the pancake and cook the other side until golden brown and completely set, about 2 minutes more.

Serve with a generous pat of butter and a dollop of goat cheese on top.

Pancakes are a much-loved morning ritual at camp (heck, even at home), but over the years I've seen far too many mixes come out of a box or even a spray can. Pancake mix is one of those things that's just too easy not to make at home, so stir up a batch of my baking mix and treat your tentmates to real, homemade, fresh, and fluffy buttermilk pancakes.

BUTTERMILK PANCAKES WITH MAPLE, MASCARPONE, AND BERRIES

MAKES 4 SERVINGS

FOR THE PANCAKES

2 cups (240 g) Multipurpose Baking Mix (page 44)

2 cups (475 ml) buttermilk

½ cup (115 g) mascarpone cheese

2 large eggs

Butter

FOR THE TOPPINGS

2 tablespoons powdered sugar

½ cup (115 g) mascarpone cheese

2 cups (150 g) raspberries, blackberries, or blueberries

Maple syrup

To make the pancakes, in a large bowl, whisk together the baking mix, buttermilk, mascarpone, and eggs until well blended.

In a small bowl, stir the powdered sugar into the other ½ cup (115 g) of mascarpone and set aside.

Heat a large skillet over medium heat and melt a pat of butter, swirling to coat the surface. Ladle ¼ cup (60 ml) batter at a time into the skillet. Cook until bubbles break on the surface and the edges of the pancake begin to set, about 3 minutes. Flip and cook the other side until golden brown and completely set, about 2 minutes more. Repeat with the remaining batter. (To keep the pancakes warm, stack and wrap them in foil as they finish cooking.)

Serve with a dollop of the sweetened mascarpone, a handful of berries, and a drizzle of maple syrup on top.

SKEWERS: TO SOAK OR NOT TO SOAK?

Conventional culinary wisdom says that wooden skewers should be soaked in water before grilling. But does this really help prevent burning? We feel this practice is up for debate—it seems that no matter how long you soak the skewers, the ends are bound to scorch a bit over a hot grill. If you're concerned about the ends of your skewers burning off completely, you can wrap them in foil or, better yet, invest in stainless steel skewers.

These breakfast kebabs are a fun take on the traditional French toast and bacon pairing. If your grill is big enough, you can even make French toast for a crowd by doubling the recipe. (Just be sure to bring enough skewers!) Make them a couple of days into your camping trip to give your bread some time to stale. If you're starting with fresh bread but want to make French toast in the morning, cut it the night before and lay the slices out to dry someplace warm and protected, like the dashboard of your car. The bread will lose just enough moisture for the ideal French toast texture.

GRILLED FRENCH TOAST AND BACON BITES

MAKES 4 SERVINGS

3 large eggs

1 cup (240 ml) half-and-half or milk

¼ cup (60 ml) spiced rum

1 tablespoon sugar

6 (¾- to 1-inch-thick) slices slightly stale challah, brioche, or country-style bread

8 strips thick-cut bacon

Maple syrup

Note: If you like your bacon smoky and sweet, brush on some maple syrup before grilling, and occasionally brush the slices with more syrup as they cook.

Prepare a grill for two-zone heat (see page 28).

In a wide, shallow dish, whisk together the eggs, half-and-half, rum, and sugar until the custard is very well blended. (You want to avoid any lingering clumps of egg yolk or egg white that will turn into cooked eggs on your French toast.)

Set aside 6 skewers until ready to use. Cut each slice of bread into 1-inch (2-cm) chunks. (You should have about 36 pieces.) Arrange the chunks in a single layer in the dish, working in batches if necessary, and soak the bread in the custard for about 10 seconds. Flip and soak the other side for about 10 seconds more until the bread is fully saturated but not falling apart. Thread the bread onto skewers and set aside to drain slightly. Thread the bacon onto the remaining skewers, folding the bacon back and forth accordion-style and piercing through the meaty parts of the bacon rather than the fat.

Grill the bacon over indirect heat, turning occasionally, for 10 to 12 minutes, until the edges are crisp and browned but the centers are still moist.

Grill the bread over direct heat, turning occasionally, for about 5 minutes, or until the surface is dry and golden brown and the centers are cooked through. If the bread is browning too quickly, finish the skewers over indirect heat once they get a good char.

Serve with a drizzle of maple syrup.

French toast is already a decadent option for the first meal of the day, so why not make it even more decadent? This recipe is almost like a PB&J for breakfast, with swirls of peanut butter slathered between two thick slices of eggy bread and served with a syrupy, jammy topping of honey-sweetened berries. Feel free to sub in your favorite nut butter in place of the peanut butter and switch up the berries for some variation.

FOR THE TOPPING

3 cups (360 g) blackberries

¼ cup (60 ml) honey

Juice of ½ medium lemon

FOR THE FRENCH TOAST

3 large eggs

1 cup (240 ml) half-and-half or milk

1 tablespoon sugar

½ to ¾ cup (125 to 200 g) peanut butter

8 (¾- to 1-inch-thick) slices slightly stale challah, brioche, or country-style bread

1 tablespoon butter

✦ MIX IT UP ✦

To take your French toast up a level, start with exceptional bread. While the dense crumb of challah makes it many a cook's favorite, you can also try a French baguette, sourdough loaf, Italian panettone bread, or even cinnamon swirl bread. (Just omit the sugar in the custard if you start with a sweet bread.) Buy a whole loaf rather than a pre-sliced one so you can cut thicker slices yourself.

PEANUT BUTTER-STUFFED FRENCH TOAST WITH HONEYED BLACKBERRIES

MAKES 4 SERVINGS

To make the topping, in a small saucepan over medium-high heat, combine the blackberries, honey, and lemon juice. Cook until the berries begin to bubble and break down, about 5 minutes, stirring frequently to prevent the mixture from boiling over. Remove the pot from the heat and cover to keep warm.

To make the French toast, whisk together the eggs, half-and-half, and sugar in a wide, shallow dish until the custard is very well blended. (You want to avoid any lingering clumps of egg yolk or egg white that will turn into cooked eggs on your French toast.) Spread the peanut butter evenly over 4 slices of the bread, then top with the remaining 4 slices. Soak the sandwiches in the custard for about 10 seconds on each side, then set them aside to drain slightly.

In a large skillet over medium heat, melt the butter and swirl to completely coat the surface. Lay the sandwiches in the skillet and cook until the bottoms are golden, 3 to 4 minutes. Flip and cook for 3 to 4 minutes more, until both sides are crisp and browned.

Spoon the warm berries and their juices on top before serving.

8 large eggs

¼ cup (60 ml) milk

¼ teaspoon kosher salt

1 tablespoon olive oil, plus more for toasting

½ medium red onion, chopped

2 medium tomatoes, diced and drained

2 tablespoons capers, drained and chopped

3 ounces (85 g) smoked salmon, chopped

½ cup (113 g) cream cheese, softened (preferably dill cream cheese)

4 (10-inch) flour tortillas

Ground black pepper

There are bagels and lox. Then there are breakfast burritos and lox, a mashup of my favorite food vessel, the ever-versatile tortilla wrap, with the classic combo beloved by New Yorkers and commuters everywhere. If you're on the move in the morning, wrap these burritos in foil to keep them warm and enjoy them en route to your destination. (Or even at your destination—the burritos can be eaten up to 2 hours after they're made.)

BREAKFAST BURRITOS AND LOX

MAKES 4 BURRITOS

In a large bowl, whisk together the eggs, milk, and salt until well blended.

Drizzle the oil in a large skillet over medium heat. Add the onion and cook until it starts to turn translucent, about 3 minutes. Add the egg mixture and cook undisturbed until it begins to set, about 2 minutes. Softly scramble the eggs until there's no longer liquid but they still look wet. Stir in the tomato, capers, and salmon and remove the skillet from the heat.

Spread 2 tablespoons of the cream cheese down the center of each tortilla. Spoon the egg mixture over the cream cheese, dividing it evenly among the tortillas, and scatter a pinch of pepper on top. Fold the sides of the tortillas up and over the mixture, then roll into burritos.

As an optional (but recommended) last step to warm and seal the burritos, wipe out the skillet with paper towels (or use a separate clean skillet) and heat over medium heat. Swirl in a little oil and arrange the burritos seam sides down in the skillet. Toast until golden brown, about 5 minutes, turning once.

✧ USE IT UP ✧

What else can you do with that of container of cream cheese? Use it up in Pinwheel Picnic Wraps (page 86).

FOOD ANTHROPOLOGY

Today, what most people refer to as lox (as in "bagels and lox") is actually Nova smoked salmon, the version commonly found in supermarkets. Also called Nova lox, Nova Scotia salmon, or simply smoked salmon (a generic term that can refer to any type of preparation), it's typically a fillet that is lightly cold-smoked after curing. The traditional Jewish brined salmon from where bagels and lox originated is actually made from the belly of salmon and has a saltier and bolder flavor.

8 large eggs

¼ cup (60 ml) milk

¼ teaspoon kosher salt, plus more for seasoning

1 cup (113 g) shredded Monterey jack, pepper jack, or sharp Cheddar cheese, divided

2 tablespoons olive oil

1 small yellow onion, finely chopped

4 cloves garlic, minced

1 poblano pepper, finely chopped

2 jalapeño peppers, minced

4 cups (120 g) corn tortilla chips, broken into 1-inch pieces, divided

2 medium tomatoes, finely chopped and drained

Ground black pepper

Handful of cilantro leaves, chopped

1 medium avocado, pitted, peeled, and sliced

Hot sauce

 MIX IT UP

Migas makes a great lazy-morning breakfast, as everyone can choose and add his or her own accompaniments for the scramble. Set out a few options such as salsa, pico de gallo, scallions, guacamole, sour cream, corn or flour tortillas, refried beans, black beans, pinto beans, and more cheese.

Two things make this recipe especially good. First, it's considered a hangover cure (or maybe it's just the easiest meal to make after a late night of whiskey-fueled stories around a campfire). Second, it happens to be a brilliant way to use up those bits of broken chips at the bottom of the bag. Better known as migas (though not the migas of Spanish origin, which is a significantly different dish), this Tex-Mex version is essentially a scramble with a kick. Eat it as is, wrap it up in tortillas, or serve it with a side of refried beans for a more belly-filling meal.

TEX-MEX SCRAMBLED EGGS WITH TORTILLA CHIPS, TOMATOES, AND CHILES

MAKES 4 SERVINGS

In a medium bowl, whisk together the eggs, milk, and salt until well blended. Stir in ½ cup (56 g) of the cheese and set aside.

In a large skillet over medium-high heat, add the oil, onion, and garlic and cook until the onion starts to turn translucent, 2 to 3 minutes. Add the poblano and jalapeño peppers and cook until tender, about 2 minutes.

Reduce the heat to medium-low and pour in the egg mixture. Scramble until curds start to form, about 3 minutes. Add two-thirds of the tortilla chips, gently stir to combine, and continue scrambling until the eggs are soft but still wet, about 3 minutes. Add the tomatoes and remaining ½ cup (56 g) cheese and cook until the eggs are softly scrambled and cooked through, about 3 minutes more. Stir in the remaining one-third tortilla chips and remove from the heat.

Season with salt and pepper to taste, garnish with cilantro, and serve with avocado and hot sauce on the side.

This autumn-inspired breakfast adds a little flair to the basic bacon-and-potato hash by marrying pancetta and sweet potatoes for a dish that's deeper yet more delicate in flavor. You can vary the texture and taste by experimenting with different varieties of sweet potatoes (such as Japanese sweet potatoes, which have hints of chestnut) and apples (ranging from sweet to tart). To make more servings (or if you just really like eggs), simply make more wells in the final step of the recipe.

SWEET POTATO, APPLE, AND PANCETTA HASH

MAKES 4 SERVINGS

6 ounces pancetta, cut into small dice

1 small yellow onion, finely chopped

2 medium apples, cored and cut into ½-inch (1-cm) dice (about 1 pound/450 g)

2 tablespoons olive oil

2 large sweet potatoes, peeled and cut into ½-inch (1-cm) dice (about 2½ pounds/1 kg)

1 teaspoon red pepper flakes

½ teaspoon kosher salt

¼ teaspoon ground black pepper

2 cups (65 g) packed baby spinach

4 large eggs

Note: In a well-stocked supermarket, pancetta can be found pre-diced and packaged in the cured meats cooler.

Heat a large skillet over medium-high heat. Add the pancetta and cook until browned and crispy, 5 to 8 minutes, stirring occasionally. Transfer the pancetta to a large plate, reserving the fat in the skillet.

Let the fat reheat for about 1 minute. Add the onion and cook until it starts to turn translucent, 2 to 3 minutes. Stir in the apples and cook until golden brown, 3 to 5 minutes. Transfer the onion and apples to the plate of pancetta.

Reheat the skillet and lightly coat the bottom with the oil. Add the sweet potatoes in a single layer and cook undisturbed until browned on the bottom, about 5 minutes. Sprinkle the red pepper flakes, salt, and pepper on top and continue cooking, stirring occasionally, for 8 to 10 minutes, or until the sweet potatoes are tender.

Return the pancetta, onion, and apples to the skillet and stir to combine. Add the spinach and cook until wilted, 2 to 3 minutes.

Using a spoon, make 4 deep wells in the mixture. Crack an egg into each well, cover the skillet, and cook until the yolks are just set, 8 to 10 minutes. (If you like your yolks less runny, poach for a few additional minutes.)

There's always that one person in camp who loves to wake with the sun, start the coffee, and slowly rouse the others from their tents with the smell of bacon wafting through the air. If that person is you, put these potatoes on the menu. They take a little longer to cook but only a few minutes to assemble, making them the perfect lazy-morning meditation. Serve them as a whole meal in themselves or as a side dish to eggs (and don't stop at breakfast, either—they go great with steaks for dinner).

BACON-WRAPPED POTATOES WITH BLUE CHEESE

MAKES 4 SERVINGS

Olive oil spray

6 strips bacon, cut in half

12 new potatoes (about 1½ pounds/680 g)

Ground black pepper

1 cup (227 g) sour cream

½ cup (56 g) crumbled blue cheese

2 scallions, thinly sliced

Milk (optional)

Prepare a mound of wood coals, hardwood lump charcoal, or charcoal briquettes (see page 28). Move about a quart's worth of coals to the cooking pit and arrange them in a ring (see pages 32 to 34).

Lightly spray a dutch oven with oil. Wrap a strip of bacon tightly around each potato and arrange the wrapped potatoes in a single layer in the oven, bacon seams down. Scatter a few pinches of pepper on top, cover, and place 2 rings of coals on the lid.

Roast over high heat for 40 to 50 minutes, until the bacon is crisp and the potatoes are tender. Replenish the coals as needed to maintain high heat and rotate the oven and lid halfway through for even cooking.

In a medium bowl, combine the sour cream, blue cheese, and scallions. If desired, add a little milk to thin the consistency. Serve as a dip or drizzle for the potatoes.

HOW DID THE DUTCH OVEN GET ITS NAME?

The term *dutch oven* has endured since the early 1700s, though its origin is somewhat of a mystery. It's commonly believed that an Englishman named Abraham Darby traveled to the Netherlands to study the more advanced Dutch process for casting metal cooking vessels. He returned to Britain and eventually developed and patented a superior method that produced thinner and lighter pots than their predecessors. It's possible his "dutch ovens" may have been named for the original Dutch process.

Another theory proposes that the name came from Dutch salesmen who brought their cast metal pots to the American colonies, and yet another suggests the name arose from the pots' popularity among the early "Dutch" (German) settlers of Pennsylvania—*Dutch* being an adaptation of the German word *Deutsch*.

Frittatas are one of those meals I affectionately call "kitchen pantry" dishes, as you can add almost anything from your kitchen (pantry or not) to a custardlike base of eggs. While traditional frittatas require flipping (or starting on the stove and finishing in the oven), a dutch oven frittata is a one-pot wonder, cooking in the same vessel, same spot. Spinach and artichokes are a classic pairing, but dig through your cooler for other add-ins that may be languishing at the end of your camping trip. Last night's leftover sausage, half an avocado, some sprigs of basil, and the odds and ends from cans and jars are all fair game.

DUTCH OVEN SPINACH AND ARTICHOKE FRITTATA

MAKES 4 SERVINGS

12 large eggs

½ cup (120 ml) milk

½ cup (56 g) shredded sharp Cheddar cheese

½ teaspoon kosher salt

Olive oil spray

2 medium shallots, sliced

4 cloves garlic, minced

3 cups (300 g) packed baby spinach

1 (14-ounce/400 g) can artichoke hearts, drained and chopped

½ cup (50 g) grated Parmesan cheese

Prepare a mound of wood coals, hardwood lump charcoal, or charcoal briquettes (see page 28). Move about half the coals to the cooking pit and arrange them in a full spread (see pages 32 to 34).

In a large bowl, lightly beat the eggs with the milk, Cheddar, and salt.

Spray a dutch oven with oil and heat it over the coals. Add the shallots and garlic to the oven and cook until the shallots start to turn translucent, about 2 minutes. Stir in the spinach and cook until wilted, 2 to 3 minutes. Add the artichokes and stir to combine.

Move the oven off the coals and arrange the coals in a ring (see pages 33 to 34). Set the oven on the coals, pour the egg mixture evenly over the vegetables, and give a quick stir to incorporate all of the ingredients. Cook undisturbed until the eggs start to set around the edges, 3 to 5 minutes. Sprinkle the Parmesan on top, cover, and place 1½ rings of coals on the lid.

Bake over medium heat until the eggs are puffy and the frittata jiggles slightly when you push on it, about 15 minutes.

Remove the oven from the heat, uncover, and let stand for 5 minutes before serving.

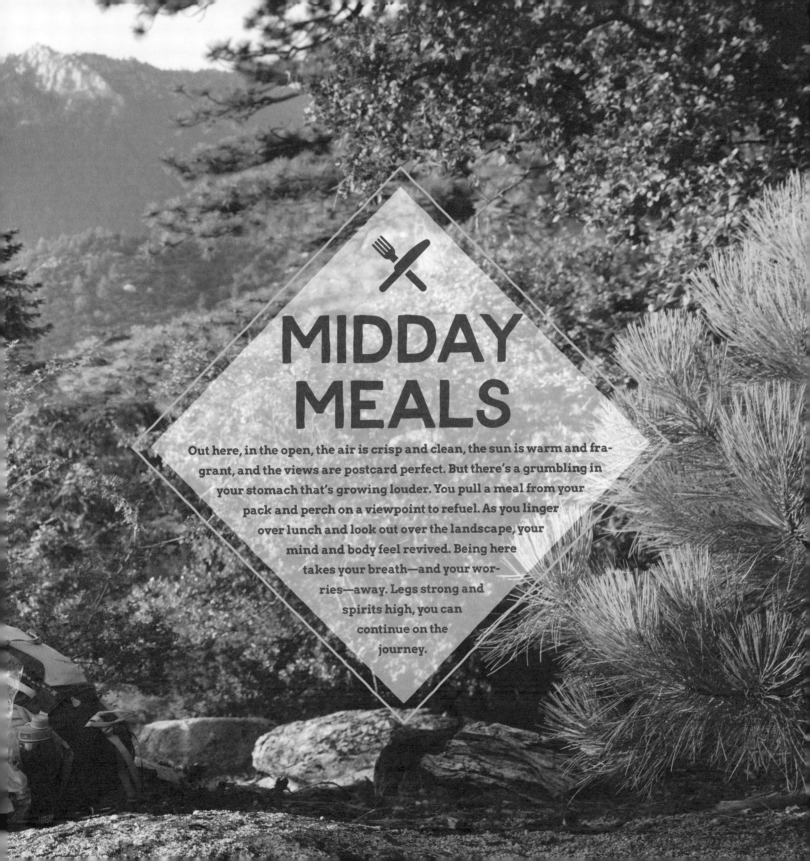

MIDDAY MEALS

Out here, in the open, the air is crisp and clean, the sun is warm and fragrant, and the views are postcard perfect. But there's a grumbling in your stomach that's growing louder. You pull a meal from your pack and perch on a viewpoint to refuel. As you linger over lunch and look out over the landscape, your mind and body feel revived. Being here takes your breath—and your worries—away. Legs strong and spirits high, you can continue on the journey.

The humble egg-in-a-hole (also known affectionately as egg-with-a-hat, egg-in-a-nest, egg-in-a-basket, and egg-in-a-frame) has been a part of American culinary history since the late 1800s. It's a delight to kids and a novelty for home cooks, and maybe that's why little has changed with the recipe as it's been passed down through generations by word of mouth. Here, it's merged with another cultural classic, the grilled cheese sandwich, for an oozy new tradition.

EGG-IN-A-HOLE GRILLED CHEESE

MAKES 4 SERVINGS

Mayonnaise

8 slices sandwich bread

1⅓ cups (150 g) shredded sharp Cheddar cheese

4 large eggs

Kosher salt and ground black pepper

Spread a thin layer of mayonnaise on half of the bread slices, then turn them over and sprinkle the cheese evenly over each slice. Top with the remaining slices of bread and coat them with a thin layer of mayonnaise.

Heat a large skillet over medium-low heat. Working in batches, place the sandwiches in the skillet and cook for about 3 minutes, until the cheese begins to melt and the bottoms are golden brown.

Flip the sandwiches. Using a 2 ½-inch (6-cm) cookie cutter or the rim of a sturdy glass, cut a hole in the center of the sandwiches. (Continue to cook the sandwich cutouts on the side of the skillet.) Crack an egg into each hole, season with a pinch of salt and pepper, and cover. Cook until the egg whites are set and the yolks are done to your liking, 3 to 5 minutes. Repeat with the remaining sandwiches.

Serve the sandwich cutouts on top of the eggs as the "hats."

If you love the simplicity of grilled cheese but just wish it had a little more oomph, give this California-inspired version a gander. Creamy avocado mashed with a smoky chile takes the classic toast up a few notches with not much more effort involved. But the real trick is on the outside: using mayo instead of butter gives the bread a beautifully brown and crunchy crust, it won't burn as easily, and it's much easier to spread. (Because who hasn't been frustrated with rock-hard butter that smushes or tears apart a slice of bread?)

CHIPOTLE CHEDDAR GRILLED CHEESE WITH MASHED AVOCADO

2 small avocados, pitted, peeled, and diced

2 canned chipotle chiles in adobo sauce, minced

Juice of 1 small lime

Mayonnaise

8 slices sourdough bread

1⅓ cups (150 g) shredded sharp Cheddar cheese

MAKES 4 SERVINGS

Prepare a grill over high heat.

In a small bowl, mash the avocados. Stir in the chiles, adobo sauce, and lime juice until well combined.

Spread a thin layer of mayonnaise on half of the bread slices, then turn them over. Top each slice with an equal amount of the avocado mixture and a sprinkle of cheese. Lay the remaining slices of bread on top and coat with a thin layer of mayonnaise.

Place the sandwiches on the grill and cook until the cheese begins to melt and the bottoms are golden brown, 3 to 4 minutes. Flip and continue cooking until the cheese is fully melted and the sandwiches are crisp and browned all over, 3 to 4 minutes more.

MAKE IT A SKILLET SANDWICH

If you don't want to fire up a grill, heat a large skillet over medium heat. Cook the sandwiches for 6 to 8 minutes, until both sides are golden brown and the cheese is completely melted, turning once.

STUFF IT

Cheese isn't the only thing you can put in your grilled cheese. Mix it up by adding sautéed mushrooms, caramelized onions, bacon and tomato, pepperoni and sun-dried tomato, bread-and-butter pickles, kimchi, or even leftover chili.

2 tablespoons olive oil

1 small yellow onion, finely chopped

4 cloves garlic, minced

6 ounces (170 g) pancetta, cut into small dice

3 tablespoons Moroccan Spice Blend (below)

1 (15-ounce/425 g) can diced tomatoes

2 (15-ounce/425 g) cans chickpeas, rinsed and drained

3 cups packed baby spinach

Juice of 1 medium lemon

A melting pot of a comfort meal, this bowl pulls inspiration from Moroccan spices, Indian curry, and Spanish espinacas con garbanzos (translated to the rather ordinary-sounding spinach and chickpeas, though the flavor is anything but ordinary). You can do like the Spanish do and serve it with sliced and toasted bread, or perhaps warm naan to sop up all the sauce, but this hearty bowl can satiate even the biggest appetites on its own.

MOROCCAN-SPICED SPINACH, CHICKPEA, AND PANCETTA BOWL

Heat a large skillet over medium-high heat and swirl in the oil. Add the onion and garlic and cook until the onion starts to turn translucent, 2 to 3 minutes. Stir in the pancetta and cook for about 5 minutes, until lightly browned. Add the spice blend and stir to coat thoroughly. Add the tomatoes, stir to combine, and simmer for about 10 minutes to let the flavors meld. Add the chickpeas and spinach, and cook until the chickpeas are heated through and the spinach is wilted, 3 to 5 minutes. Stir in the lemon juice.

Moroccan Spice Blend

This curry-style blend of spices takes after ras el hanout, a staple in North African cooking. It adds a warm, pungent flavor to chicken, lamb, potatoes, rice, root vegetables, and couscous.

MAKES ¼ CUP (25 G)

1 tablespoon ground cumin

1 tablespoon ground coriander

1 tablespoon ground ginger

1 teaspoon ground cinnamon

1 teaspoon smoked paprika

½ teaspoon ground cayenne pepper

½ teaspoon ground turmeric

Combine all of the ingredients in a small bowl. Transfer to a resealable plastic bag or lidded container and store in a dry, cool place for up to 6 months.

FOR THE SOUP

1 tablespoon olive oil

½ medium yellow onion, chopped

4 cloves garlic, minced

2 (28-ounce/800 g) cans crushed tomatoes

¼ cup (56 g) butter

2 teaspoons sugar, plus more to taste

¼ teaspoon kosher salt

¼ teaspoon ground black pepper

Handful of fresh basil leaves, chopped

Grated Parmesan cheese

FOR THE GRILLED CHEESE

Mayonnaise

8 slices sourdough bread

Dijon mustard

1⅓ cups (150 g) shredded sharp Cheddar cheese

If tomato soup is high on your list of perfect comfort foods, it's worth it to make your own in camp. (And it's easy!) The key to really good tomato soup is, not surprisingly, really good tomatoes. Start with quality canned organic tomatoes with a good balance of acidity and sweetness, and little more is needed to nurture them on the stove. Because no tomato soup is complete without melt-in-your-mouth grilled cheese, this one is topped with crisp and cheesy chunks of the classic sandwich for a fun take on "croutons."

TOMATO SOUP WITH GRILLED CHEESE CROUTONS

MAKES 4 SERVINGS

To make the soup, in a stockpot over medium-high heat, drizzle the oil. Add the onion and garlic and cook until the onion starts to turn translucent, 2 to 3 minutes. Pour in the tomatoes and bring to a simmer, stirring frequently to avoid splattering. Stir in the butter until it melts. Add the sugar and a hefty pinch of salt and pepper. Taste, and adjust the seasonings as needed. Reduce the heat, cover, and simmer the soup while you prepare the grilled cheese.

To make the grilled cheese, spread a thin layer of mayonnaise on half of the bread slices, then turn them over and coat with a thin layer of mustard. Sprinkle the cheese evenly over the mustard. Top with the remaining slices of bread and coat with a thin layer of mayonnaise.

Heat a large skillet over medium-low heat. Place the sandwiches in the skillet and cook until the cheese begins to melt and the bottoms are golden brown, about 3 minutes. Turn them over and cook until the cheese is fully melted and the bread is crisp and browned all over, about 3 minutes more.

Transfer the sandwiches to a cutting board and cut each sandwich into 1-inch (2-cm) chunks. Remove the soup from the heat and stir in the basil. Divide the soup among 4 bowls and top with a handful of grated Parmesan and grilled cheese "croutons."

When the days begin to shorten, the weather starts to cool, and you can't shake off that late-morning chill in camp, pull out the soup pot and put this soul-warming chowder on to simmer. Velvety sweet potatoes, silky quinoa, and creamy feta add richness to an otherwise simple bowl of comfort that has autumn written all over it. Stash a steamy serving of it in a leak-proof insulated container and take it with you on that afternoon outing in the canoe.

SPINACH, SWEET POTATO, AND CARROT QUINOA CHOWDER

MAKES 6 SERVINGS

2 tablespoons olive oil

1 small yellow onion, chopped

4 cloves garlic, minced

¼ teaspoon red pepper flakes

1 medium sweet potato, peeled and cut into small dice (about ½ pound/226 g)

4 new potatoes, cut into small dice (about ½ pound/226 g)

1 medium carrot, thinly sliced

5 cups (12 dL) chicken broth

1 cup (177 g) uncooked quinoa

2 cups (150 g) packed baby spinach

4 ounces (113 g) feta cheese, finely chopped

Ground black pepper

Heat a stockpot over medium-high heat and swirl in the oil. Add the onion, garlic, and red pepper flakes and cook until the onion starts to turn translucent, 2 to 3 minutes. Stir in the sweet potatoes, potatoes, and carrot and cook until the vegetables start to soften, 5 to 8 minutes, stirring occasionally. Add the broth and quinoa and bring to a boil. Reduce the heat and simmer until the vegetables are tender and the quinoa is cooked through, 15 to 20 minutes. (Quinoa is fully cooked when the tiny spirals, or the germ, are separated from and curled around the seeds.)

Stir in the spinach and feta and continue cooking until the spinach is wilted and the cheese is melted, 2 to 3 minutes. Season with pepper to taste.

Note: Buy block feta packed in brine, which is fresher and creamier than pre-crumbled feta.

Hot. Sweet. Tart. Crunchy. This vibrant Thai-inspired salad has a lot of things going for it in the flavor and texture departments. Fresh raw vegetables keep it light and crisp, while tender quinoa makes it substantial enough to be a meal on its own. A generous handful of fresh herbs packs a taste bud–tingling punch that's elevated even more by the spicy dressing.

THAI QUINOA SALAD WITH A TRIO OF FRESH HERBS

MAKES 4 TO 6 SERVINGS

FOR THE DRESSING

2 tablespoons fish sauce

2 tablespoons toasted sesame oil

2 tablespoons packed brown sugar

1 tablespoon sriracha

1 tablespoon minced ginger

2 cloves garlic, minced

Juice of 6 medium limes

At Home

To make the dressing, whisk all of the ingredients in a small bowl until the sugar is dissolved and the ingredients are well blended. Transfer to a lidded container and chill for up to 3 days.

You can also save some time in camp by packing precooked quinoa in a cooler, as the salad is quite refreshing when served chilled.

RECIPE CONTINUES

FOR THE SALAD

3¾ (890 ml) cups water

1 teaspoon kosher salt

2 cups (354 g) uncooked quinoa

1 large carrot, shredded or cut into matchsticks

1 medium bell pepper, cut into thin strips

1 medium English cucumber, cut into small dice (see Note)

4 scallions, chopped

½ cup (25 g) chopped cilantro leaves

½ cup (25 g) chopped fresh mint leaves

½ cup (25 g) chopped fresh basil leaves (preferably Thai basil)

Note: English cucumbers are the long and slender varieties wrapped in plastic in the produce aisle. If you're unable to source them, any thin-skinned seedless cucumber will work for this recipe.

In Camp

To make the salad, bring the water and salt to a boil in a small saucepan. Stir in the quinoa. Reduce the heat, cover, and simmer for about 15 minutes, until all of the liquid is absorbed and the quinoa is tender. (Quinoa is fully cooked when the tiny spirals, or the germ, are separated from and curled around the seeds.) Remove the saucepan from the heat and let stand, covered, for 5 minutes. Transfer the quinoa to a large bowl, fluff with a fork, and let cool.

Add the carrot, bell pepper, cucumber, scallion, cilantro, mint, and basil to the quinoa in the bowl. Pour in the dressing and toss to coat.

✧ MIX IT UP ✧

Experiment with other vegetables in the salad for different flavors and textures, such as shelled edamame, grape tomatoes, and baby greens. If you have leftover cooked chicken from last night's dinner, shred it up and toss it in with the vegetables and herbs.

✧ USE IT UP ✧

Before you toss out that last bit of cilantro, use it up in Grilled Guacamole (page 106), Mexican Shrimp Cocktail (page 123), Mexican Street Corn Salad (page 122), Grilled Shrimp Tacos with Corn and Tomato Salsa (page 98), Market-Fresh Taco Salad with Creamy Cilantro-Lime Dressing (page 80), Foil-Pack Salmon with Pineapple Salsa (page 101), Red Lentil Soup with Carrot and Cumin (page 138), or Cuban Rice with Chicken (page 167).

GOES-WITH-EVERYTHING GRILLING SAUCE

Every camp cook needs a secret sauce up his or her sleeve, and this versatile sauce is the kind of thing you want in your grilling pantry. It tingles all the taste buds with a trio of salty, sweet, and sour notes and complements everything you put on (or take off) the grill. Use it as a drizzle or dip; as a marinade for tender vegetables like porto-bello mushrooms, eggplant, and zucchini; or for proteins like chicken, steak, and tofu. Brush the sauce on the food as it's cooking to keep it moist, or glaze it once it's off the grill to enhance its flavor. Whatever you do, just make sure you're never without these three simple ingredients.

MAKES 1 CUP (240 ML)

⅓ cup (80 ml) soy sauce

⅓ cup (80 ml) honey

⅓ cup (80 ml) lemon juice

Combine all of the ingredients in a small bowl. Transfer to a lidded container and chill for up to 3 days.

If you grow your own vegetables or love to visit farmers' markets, this recipe is calling your name. It's summertime alfresco dining at its finest, meant to be shared family-style, with quality ingredients prepared simply over the smoke of a grill. Use a kaleidoscope of colorful produce (everything from tomatoes to carrots, radicchio to eggplant) and take the feast into the night by stringing up lights and adding a few meats to the grill as well. Speckled with char and piled on a platter, the production is guaranteed to look impressive—even if it took only minutes to make.

PILE OF GRILLED MARKET VEGETABLES WITH HERBED TOASTS

MAKES 4 SERVINGS

8 ounces (226 g) goat cheese, softened

½ cup (120 ml) milk or half-and-half

Handful of mixed fresh herbs, minced (such as parsley, chives, thyme, and rosemary)

4 pounds (2 kg) mixed vegetables, prepared according to *The Go-To Guide for Grilling Vegetables* on page 81

Olive oil spray

Kosher salt and ground black pepper

1 cup (240 ml) Goes-with-Everything Grilling Sauce (page 78)

1 loaf Italian, French, or sourdough bread, sliced

½ cup (113 g) Garlic-Herb Butter, softened (page 161)

Prepare a grill for high heat.

In a small bowl, whisk the goat cheese, milk, and herbs until light, fluffy, and well blended. Set aside until ready to serve.

Lightly spray the vegetables with oil, season with a few pinches of salt and pepper, and place the vegetables on the grill in batches. Cook until charred all over with good grill marks, turning frequently. Remove each vegetable from the grill as it is cooked and transfer to a serving dish. Drizzle the sauce over the vegetables. (Alternatively, you can serve the sauce on the side in dipping bowls.)

Grill the bread until golden brown on both sides, 2 to 3 minutes, turning once.

To serve, pile the vegetables and toasts in the center of the table and offer the herb butter and herb-whipped goat cheese for spreading.

✧ MIX IT UP ✧

If you have leftover grilled vegetables, turn them into lunch the next day. Stuff the vegetables (no need to reheat them) into pita pockets or tortilla wraps dressed with leftover herbed goat cheese, Easy Aioli (page 91), hummus, or vinaigrette.

FOR THE DRESSING

1 cup (50 g) packed cilantro

½ cup (113 g) sour cream

¼ cup (56 g) mayonnaise

2 tablespoons cider vinegar

2 cloves garlic

½ teaspoon kosher salt

¼ teaspoon ground
black pepper

Juice of 1 medium lime

½ cup (120 ml) olive oil

FOR THE SALAD

1 medium head romaine
lettuce, chopped

1 (15-ounce/425 g) can pinto
beans, rinsed and drained

1 cup (150 g) halved
cherry tomatoes

2 ears corn, shucked and
kernels removed

1 bunch radishes,
quartered, greens reserved
and chopped

2 small avocados, pitted,
peeled, and diced

1 medium bell pepper, cored
and diced

½ medium red onion, diced

Handful of cilantro
leaves, chopped

Crumbled Cotija cheese

Tortilla chips

You might think a taco salad isn't a taco salad without the meat, but I promise you won't miss it in this vegetable-laden version full of fresh market finds. Corn kernels are left raw in this recipe, and if you've never eaten corn that wasn't cooked in some way, you're in for a treat. Look for the freshest ears of young corn in season, and you'll be blown away by how sweet, tender, and almost milky they taste in their natural state. If you can find radishes with a vibrant, healthy head of greens still attached, use the greens as well. Once you've assembled the cast of characters, a creamy, zesty, herby dressing pulls it all together for this light but filling lunch.

MARKET-FRESH TACO SALAD WITH CREAMY CILANTRO-LIME DRESSING

MAKES 4 SERVINGS

At Home

To make the dressing, add the cilantro, sour cream, mayonnaise, vinegar, garlic, salt, pepper, and lime juice to the bowl of a food processor. Pulse until well blended, scraping down the sides of the bowl as needed. Run the processor and pour the oil through the feeding tube in a steady stream until the dressing is smooth and emulsified. Transfer the dressing to a lidded container and chill for up to 3 days.

In Camp

To make the salad, in a large bowl, combine the lettuce, beans, tomatoes, corn kernels, radishes, radish greens, avocados, bell pepper, onion, and cilantro. Pour in the dressing and toss to coat. Serve with a generous sprinkle of Cotija and a pile of tortilla chips on the side.

The Go-To Guide for Grilling Vegetables

Vegetables come alive on the grill as the high heat concentrates their natural sugars, making them bolder and sweeter. They're an easy way to add some side options to seared steaks and other meats, as everything can cook on the grill at once, leaving you with less mess to clean up. Coat them in the same marinade or glaze as your meats, or top them with one of the compound butters on page 160. For simple grilled vegetables, just pack some olive oil spray.

Prepare a grill over medium-high heat.

Mist the vegetable with oil and place on the grill. Cook until tender and lightly charred with crisp edges and good grill marks, turning occasionally. (For specific times, follow the chart as a general guideline. Ranges in times allow for grilling the vegetable to your preferred doneness, from crisp-tender to fork-tender.)

Vegetable	Preparation Method	Approximate Grilling Time
Asparagus	Trim tough ends	5 minutes
Bell pepper	Halve lengthwise	5 to 8 minutes
Cabbage	Cut lengthwise into eighths	6 to 8 minutes
Carrot (no more than ¾ inch in diameter)	Cut in half lengthwise	10 to 15 minutes
Corn on the cob	Shuck corn cobs; if desired, wrap in aluminum foil with a few pats of butter	8 to 10 minutes
Eggplant	Cut globe varieties into ½-inch-thick rounds; cut Chinese or Japanese varieties in half lengthwise	8 to 10 minutes
Fennel	Trim tough stems and cut bulb into quarters lengthwise	10 to 15 minutes
Lettuce (romaine)	Cut in half lengthwise	6 to 8 minutes
Mushroom (portobello)	Trim tough stem	10 to 15 minutes
Onion	Cut in half lengthwise, leaving root end intact	5 to 10 minutes
Radicchio	Cut lengthwise into quarters	6 to 8 minutes
Scallion and spring onion	Leave whole	3 to 5 minutes
Snap bean	Leave whole	5 to 8 minutes
Summer squash (crookneck, pattypan, zucchini)	Leave smaller squash (less than 1 inch in diameter) whole; cut larger squash in half lengthwise	10 to 15 minutes
Tomatoes	Cut into ½-inch-thick slices	5 minutes

Many of my favorite meals at camp are the simplest ones, needing little more than the smoke and char of a wood-fired grill for deep and savory flavor. This is as easy as it gets for a midday meal when you're famished from a morning hike and don't want to fuss too much in the kitchen. Just throw a few things on the grill, stir together a two-ingredient dressing, and sit back and celebrate the latest peak you just bagged. Any type of smoked sausage can be used in this recipe, though the spicy kick of andouille (a Louisiana-style hot sausage) pairs well with the sweet and tangy dressing.

GRILLED SAUSAGE, PEPPER, AND ONION MEDLEY

MAKES 4 SERVINGS

¼ cup (60 ml) balsamic vinegar

2 tablespoons honey

4 smoked sausages, halved lengthwise (about 12 ounces/340 g)

3 large bell peppers, cored and halved lengthwise

1 large red onion, halved lengthwise, root end left intact

Prepare a grill for medium-high heat.

In a small bowl, combine the vinegar and honey and set aside.

Place the sausages, peppers, and onion on the grill and cook for about 5 minutes on each side, until the sausage is heated through and the vegetables are crisp-tender.

Slice the peppers and onion lengthwise into strips, then divide the vegetables and sausages among 4 plates. Drizzle with the vinaigrette before serving.

 **MIX IT UP**

Serve everything over a bed of baby greens (which will wilt beautifully from the residual heat of the meat and vegetables) or toss a few slices of buttered bread on the grill and serve them on the side. (Try one of the compound butters on page 160.)

Lettuce cups are one of those things that look like special-occasion treats, but in reality they're one of the simplest recipes to whip up in the kitchen. Most of the work here—and the mess—is at home, and store-bought sauces for dipping and drizzling are worthy shortcuts when the filling itself is so good. Serve these lettuce cups at camp as an appetizer, a salad, or a main event, and let friends and family assemble the wraps themselves.

LETTUCE CUPS WITH SESAME-SOY CHICKEN

MAKES 4 SERVINGS

1 pound (450 g) boneless skinless chicken thighs

4 scallions, finely chopped

¼ cup (60 ml) soy sauce

2 tablespoons rice vinegar

1 tablespoon sesame oil

1 tablespoon grated ginger

2 tablespoons olive oil

½ medium red onion, finely chopped

4 cloves garlic, minced

3 medium cremini mushrooms, chopped

1 tablespoon hoisin sauce, plus more for serving (see Note)

1 large head butter lettuce (about ¾ pound/340 g)

1 cup (142 g) dry-roasted peanuts, chopped

Sweet chili sauce (see Note)

Sriracha

Note: Hoisin sauce and sweet chili sauce can be found near other Asian condiments in most well-stocked supermarkets.

At Home

Cut the chicken into 2-inch (5-cm) chunks and place in the bowl of a food processor. Pulse until the chicken is ground into a fine texture, scraping down the sides of the bowl as needed. (Alternatively, you can mince the chicken by hand or buy dark meat ground chicken from the butcher.)

Place the ground chicken in a large bowl. Add the scallions, soy sauce, vinegar, sesame oil, and ginger and toss to coat thoroughly. Transfer the chicken and marinade to a resealable plastic bag, squeeze out the excess air, and chill for at least 1 hour and up to 24 hours.

In Camp

Heat a large skillet over medium-high heat and swirl in the olive oil. Add the onion and garlic and cook until the onion starts to turn translucent, 2 to 3 minutes. Stir in the mushrooms and hoisin sauce and cook until the mushrooms are tender, about 2 minutes. Add the chicken and cook until golden brown, 5 to 8 minutes, stirring occasionally.

Separate the lettuce into individual leaves. Spoon equal amounts of chicken onto the lettuce and sprinkle with the peanuts. Serve with hoisin sauce, sweet chili sauce, and sriracha on the table for dipping or drizzling.

Tired of the usual turkey and cheese sandwiches? These Armenian-inspired pinwheel wraps, known as aram sandwiches or Hye rollers ("Hye" being the Armenian word for Armenian), are the answer to that inevitable question of "What's for lunch?" after the crew comes back to camp from a morning dip in the lake. The colorful and playful rolls appeal to kids and adults alike, and they make great party food as well as trail sustenance. You can fill them with an assortment of deli-style meats and vegetables, or even swap the cream cheese for other spreads, such as pesto, hummus, or Easy Aioli (page 91).

PINWHEEL PICNIC WRAPS

MAKES 4 WRAPS

1 cup (227 g) cream cheese, softened

2 scallions, thinly sliced

4 (8-by-10-inch/20-by-25-cm) sheets lavash bread (see Note)

8 ounces (226 g) thinly sliced smoked turkey breast

2 cups (66 g) packed baby spinach

2 medium tomatoes, thinly sliced

1 medium cucumber, thinly sliced

In a small bowl, combine the cream cheese and scallions.

Place each sheet of lavash on your work surface with its longest edge positioned horizontally. Spread one-fourth of the cream cheese mixture evenly over its surface. Starting at the edge closest to you, arrange one-fourth of the turkey along its length, followed by one-fourth of the spinach above the turkey, one-fourth of the tomatoes above the spinach, and one-fourth of the cucumber above the tomatoes. (Spacing the ingredients out this way, rather than layering them on top of one another, allows each roll in the pinwheel to show a different color for the most eye-catching effect. If you prefer to layer the ingredients sandwich-style, that's acceptable as well.) Roll the lavash away from you into a long, tight cylinder. Seal the edge with a little cream cheese to help the roll stay together.

To serve, slice each roll in half (or in shorter lengths if serving as finger food).

Note: Lavash is an Armenian cracker bread. Traditional lavash calls for moistening the cracker and wrapping with a damp towel until it softens. However, many deli counters and specialty grocers now carry sheets of lavash that are soft, thin, pliable, and ready for wrapping. If you're unable to find lavash, you can substitute another soft flatbread or use 10-inch (25-cm) flour tortillas.

When you need a quick and satisfying meal at camp but don't want to fire up the stove, these Mediterranean-inspired wraps are just the thing. Made from a handful of prepared ingredients you can easily pick up at the store en route to your campsite, they take little effort but offer big flavor—not to mention they travel well. Make a batch ahead of a hike, wrap tightly in plastic, and enjoy them at the viewpoint.

MEDITERRANEAN HUMMUS WRAPS WITH ROASTED RED PEPPERS, ARTICHOKES, AND FETA

MAKES 4 WRAPS

4 (10-inch/25-cm) spinach tortillas

½ cup (125 g) store-bought hummus

2 cups (66 g) packed baby spinach

¼ small red onion, sliced

3 ounces (85 g) feta cheese, sliced

6 marinated artichoke hearts, quartered

2 marinated roasted red bell peppers, sliced

Balsamic vinegar

On each tortilla, spread equal amounts of the hummus down the center, followed by the spinach, onion, feta, artichokes, and peppers. Finish with a drizzle of vinegar. Fold the sides of the tortillas up and over the filling, then roll the tortilla away from you. Slice in half and serve.

When you need to make sandwiches for a crowd, assembling ribbons of Italian cold cuts on a whole loaf is sure to impress your hungry campmates. Don't be put off by the seemingly long list of ingredients here; you're not simply making a sandwich, you're building one. Start with a good loaf of bread and quality cured meats, and the rest of the fixings can be swapped on a whim. Like some spice? Try soppressata. Love fresh herbs? Add a few handfuls of basil.

GRILLED ITALIAN LOAF WITH CAPOCOLLO, SALAMI, PROSCIUTTO, AND PROVOLONE

MAKES 4 SERVINGS

1 medium bell pepper, cored and halved lengthwise

1 loaf Italian bread (about 14 inches long)

⅓ cup (75 g) Pesto Aioli (page 91)

3 ounces (85 g) thinly sliced provolone cheese

3 ounces (85 g) thinly sliced capocollo (see Note)

3 ounces (85 g) thinly sliced Genoa salami (see Note)

3 ounces (85 g) thinly sliced prosciutto (see Note)

2 medium tomatoes, thinly sliced

¼ small red onion, thinly sliced

Olive oil

Red wine vinegar

Ground black pepper

Dried oregano

Prepare a grill for medium-high heat.

Grill the bell pepper until crisp-tender with grill marks on both sides, about 4 minutes, turning once. Transfer the bell pepper to a cutting board and cut into long, thin strips.

Cut the bread in half horizontally and lay the halves on your work surface, cut sides up. Spread the aioli evenly over the bottom half. Arrange the cheese over the aioli and top with the capocollo, salami, prosciutto, tomatoes, bell pepper, and onion. Drizzle with a little oil and vinegar, season with a hefty pinch of pepper and oregano, and lay the top half of the bread over the filling.

Wrap the sandwich tightly in aluminum foil. Grill until the bread is toasted and the sandwich is heated through, 5 to 10 minutes, turning frequently. Cut the sandwich into quarters and serve warm.

Note: Italian cold cuts are best bought from a quality market or Italian deli; ask the butcher to thinly slice the meats for you. If you're sourcing from a well-stocked supermarket, look for packaged, pre-sliced cured meats near the deli department. Capocollo is sometimes labeled as coppa or capicola.

Easy Aioli

Aioli—a name that means "oil and garlic"—is a creamy condiment from the southern French region of Provence. Though it's typically made from scratch by whisking garlic into olive oil, egg yolks, lemon juice, and mustard, store-bought mayonnaise is a clever cheat for creating your own flavored aioli to spread on burgers and sandwiches, or use as a dip for grilled vegetables and seafood. It also has a longer shelf life in the fridge than from-scratch aioli.

This shortcut aioli is easy enough to make in camp, but is best made at home and chilled overnight to let the flavors fully develop.

This is the master recipe for all the aioli variations following it.

MAKES 1 CUP (226 G)

1 cup (226 g) mayonnaise

2 cloves garlic, crushed

1 tablespoon lemon juice

½ teaspoon kosher salt

Stir together all of the ingredients in a small bowl until well combined. Transfer to a lidded container and chill for up to 2 weeks.

Variations

Herb Aioli: Add ½ cup (25 g) minced fresh herbs (such as basil, cilantro, parsley, thyme, oregano, and/or chives).

Dijon Aioli: Add 2 tablespoons Dijon mustard.

Pesto Aioli: Add 2 tablespoons homemade or store-bought pesto.

Horseradish Aioli: Add 2 tablespoons prepared horseradish.

Chipotle Aioli: Add 2 minced canned chipotle chiles in adobo sauce.

Sriracha Aioli: Add 2 tablespoons sriracha.

Every September during the grape harvest, bakeries in central Italy are filled with schiacciata all'uva, a traditional Italian flatbread (what Americans know as focaccia) seasoned with rosemary and dotted with sweet, ripe wine grapes. Most of us aren't lucky enough to travel to Tuscany during that time, so let's pull inspiration from the region with this campside spin using store-bought pita pockets, regular red grapes, and a pair of pungent, melty cheeses. If you have extra grapes on hand, throw those on the grill as well; the heat brings out an almost syrupy sweetness in the fruit that makes them perfect for snacking with cheese, salami, or simply on their own. (You'll need a portable grill with a cover for this recipe.)

GRILLED GRAPE AND GORGONZOLA PITA PIZZAS

MAKES 4 PITA PIZZAS

1 small bunch seedless red grapes (about ½ pound/226 g)

Olive oil spray

4 (6-inch/15-cm) pita breads

1 cup (113 g) crumbled Gorgonzola cheese

½ cup (56 g) shredded fontina cheese

½ teaspoon chopped fresh rosemary

½ cup (56 g) chopped walnuts

Prepare a grill for medium heat.

Mist the grapes with oil and place the clusters on the grill. Cook until soft and singed all over, 4 to 6 minutes, turning occasionally. Transfer to a cutting board and slice the larger grapes in half for easy topping.

Lay the pitas on a work surface and lightly spray both sides with oil. On each pita, scatter an equal amount of Gorgonzola, fontina, rosemary, walnuts, and grapes.

Place the pizzas on the grill, cover, and cook for 5 to 7 minutes, until the cheese is melted and the crust is crisp and browned.

 ✧ **USE IT UP** ✧

Fresh rosemary adds a really nice depth of flavor to the dish, so I don't recommend you skip it. Instead, use the rest of your rosemary in Bacon-Wrapped Trout Stuffed with Fresh Herbs (page 000), Spiced and Herbed Mixed Nuts (page 103), or the herb-whipped goat cheese in Pile of Grilled Market Vegetables with Herbed Toasts (page 79).

Make Your Own Flatbread

Did you know you can quickly and easily make your own pita pockets in camp? All you need is a batch of pizza dough and a hot skillet for these pillowy flatbreads.

MAKES 8 PITAS

1 pound (450 g) Homemade Pizza Dough (page 146)

Olive oil spray

Bring the chilled dough to room temperature for about 30 minutes.

Meanwhile, mist a square of aluminum foil with oil and place it on your work surface, oiled side up. Mist another sheet of foil with oil and set aside.

Divide the dough into 8 equal sections. Shape each section into a smooth ball and flatten into a thick disk. Place each disk on the sheet of foil and lay the second sheet of foil, oiled side down, over the disks. Using the side of a wine bottle or Nalgene bottle, roll the disk out ⅛ to ¼ inch (3 to 6 mm) thick and 7 to 8 inches (18 to 20 cm) in diameter. Reapply a fine mist of oil to the foil to prevent sticking.

Heat a large skillet over medium-high heat. Working with one pita at a time, place the dough in the skillet and cook for about 30 seconds, until bubbles start to form on the surface. Flip and cook for about 1 minute, until brown spots start to appear on the bottom. Flip again and cook for about 1 minute, until the pita is puffed and toasted all over.

If not serving immediately, store the pitas in a resealable plastic bag for up to 3 days. They can be warmed in a skillet before using.

These tacos are what I playfully dub bánh mì tacos—bánh mì being the specialty sandwich of Vietnam. I grew up on the cultural classic and fondly remember my mother slipping a homemade bánh mì in my lunchbox every morning for years. Later on, it became my mission through college to find bánh mì as savory, juicy, and crisp as the ones I remembered from my childhood. Now that I live in California, where Vietnamese cuisine is abundant, authentic bánh mì is tied with another regional staple: Mexican food. These tacos are the love child of Vietnamese and Mexican street food, and the filling of seasoned grilled pork, crunchy sweet pickles, cilantro, cucumber, and chiles will make you a believer in this culinary mashup.

VIETNAMESE PORK TACOS WITH PICKLED CARROTS AND DAIKON

MAKES 4 SERVINGS

FOR THE PICKLES

¼ pound (113 g) carrots, cut into 2-inch matchsticks (see Note)

¼ pound (113 g) daikon, cut into 2-inch matchsticks (see Note)

1 teaspoon kosher salt

⅔ cup (160 ml) white vinegar

⅔ cup (160 ml) water

2 tablespoons sugar

Note: Carrot and daikon pickles are known as *đồ chua* and can be found in most Vietnamese or Chinese markets, already prepared in jars or tubs. If you make your own, daikon radish is readily available in many Asian markets and specialty markets.

At Home

Make the pickles at least 1 day before serving them. In a colander, toss the carrots and daikon with the salt and let drain in a sink for about 30 minutes. Shake them up periodically to expel as much liquid as possible.

Meanwhile, stir the vinegar, water, and sugar in a small bowl until the sugar is dissolved.

Rinse the carrots and daikon under running water to remove excess salt, then transfer to a lidded container. Pour the brine over the vegetables and chill for up to 2 weeks.

To marinate the pork, combine the oil, sugar, fish sauce, pepper, shallots, and garlic in a large bowl. Add the pork and toss to coat thoroughly. Transfer the pork and marinade to a resealable plastic bag, squeeze out the excess air, and chill for at least 2 hours and up to 24 hours.

RECIPE CONTINUES

FOR THE MARINATED PORK

¼ cup (60 ml) toasted sesame oil

¼ cup (50 g) sugar

2 tablespoons fish sauce

1 tablespoon ground black pepper

2 medium shallots, minced

4 cloves garlic, minced

1½ pounds (680 g) pork shoulder, thinly sliced into 1-inch-wide (2-cm-wide) strips (see Note)

FOR THE TACOS

12 (5-inch/12-cm) tortillas, warmed

1 bunch cilantro, chopped

1 medium cucumber, cut into 3-inch spears

3 jalapeño or serrano peppers, thinly sliced

Mayonnaise or Sriracha Aioli (page 91)

In Camp

Prepare a grill over medium heat.

Thread the pork onto skewers and grill until charred and caramelized all over, 6 to 8 minutes, turning frequently. Transfer the pork to a cutting board and chop into bite-size pieces.

Stage a taco bar by arranging the pork, pickled carrots and daikon, tortillas, cilantro, cucumber, jalapeños, and mayonnaise on a table, and let guests assemble their own tacos.

Note: If you're finding it difficult to slice the pork shoulder, freeze it slightly to firm up the meat. Alternatively, you can ask your butcher to cut the slab into ¼-inch (6-mm) slices.

KITCHEN HACK

Carry raw meats from the prep table to the grill on a foil-lined cutting board. Once the meat is on the grill, discard the foil and you have a clean surface to put (and cut) the cooked meat on without having to wash it first.

Grilled seasoned shrimp is a lighter, but no less delicious, alternative to heavier and meatier taco fillings, and the charred corn and tomato salsa is a snazzy variation for camp (or home—who says you can't make this for Taco Tuesday for the family as well?). Either way, because everyone loves a good taco bar, set the food out as the skewers come off the grill, add a few additional fixings if you have 'em (sliced avocado, sour cream or crema Mexicana, a bottle of hot sauce), and let your friends and family go to town. The only thing missing from this recipe is an ice-cold beer—but you've probably got that covered.

GRILLED SHRIMP TACOS WITH CORN AND TOMATO SALSA

MAKES 4 SERVINGS

FOR THE TACOS

1¾ pounds (800 g) large shrimp, peeled and deveined (16/20 count)

2 tablespoons olive oil

4 teaspoons South-of-the-Border Seasoning (page 175)

12 (5-inch/12-cm) tortillas, warmed

2 medium limes, cut into wedges

At Home

To marinate the shrimp for the tacos, add the shrimp, oil, and seasoning to a large bowl and toss to coat thoroughly. Transfer the shrimp to a resealable plastic bag, squeeze out the excess air, and chill for at least 1 hour and up to 24 hours.

RECIPE CONTINUES

FOR THE SALSA

2 ears corn, shucked

2 medium tomatoes, finely chopped

½ medium red onion, finely chopped

1 jalapeño pepper, minced

3 cloves garlic, minced

Handful of cilantro leaves, chopped

Juice of 2 medium limes

Kosher salt and ground black pepper

In Camp

Prepare a grill over high heat.

To make the salsa, place the corn on the grill and cook until just tender and charred on all sides, 6 to 8 minutes, turning the cobs every 2 minutes. Transfer the corn to a cutting board and let cool slightly. Shave the kernels off the cobs with a knife.

In a serving bowl, combine the corn kernels, tomatoes, onion, jalapeño, garlic, cilantro, and lime juice. Season with salt and pepper to taste.

Thread the shrimp onto skewers and grill until opaque and well charred, about 5 minutes, turning once. Pull the shrimp off the skewers into a serving dish.

Stage a taco bar by arranging the shrimp, salsa, tortillas, and lime wedges on a table, and let guests assemble their own tacos.

TORTILLA TIP

To quickly warm tortillas and impart a little smoke, throw them on the grill and heat each side until small brown spots appear. Transfer the tortillas to a sheet of aluminum foil and cover with a second sheet of foil. Stack the tortillas as you take them off the grill and wrap them tightly with foil until ready to serve. Alternatively, you can make small stacks of five or fewer tortillas, wrap them in foil, and heat them on the grill for a few minutes, turning occasionally, until the packet is warmed through.

USE IT UP

If you're looking for more ways you can use cilantro, make Grilled Guacamole (page 106), Mexican Shrimp Cocktail (page 123), Mexican Street Corn Salad (page 122), Thai Quinoa Salad with a Trio of Fresh Herbs (page 75), Market-Fresh Taco Salad with Creamy Cilantro-Lime Dressing (page 80), Red Lentil Soup with Carrot and Cumin (page 138), Foil-Pack Salmon with Pineapple Salsa (page 101), or Cuban Rice with Chicken (page 167).

Light and tangy pineapple salsa adds tropical flair to foil-baked salmon fillets, making it feel like you're sunning yourself on an island even if you're sitting in your flannel in the middle of the woods. When warmed over the grill, the juices seep into the fish, making every bite feel like a big fat taste of summer. Bonus: This recipe makes extra salsa that you can serve on the side or save for a snack later in the day.

FOIL-PACK SALMON WITH PINEAPPLE SALSA

FOR THE SALSA

1 small pineapple, cored and cut into small dice (about 3 pounds/1,360 g; see Note)

1 serrano pepper, minced

½ small red onion, finely chopped

Handful of cilantro, chopped

Juice of 1 large lime

Kosher salt and ground black pepper

Note: If you don't want to cut up a whole pineapple in camp, use packaged diced pineapple or canned pineapple chunks from the grocery store. You'll need about 2½ cups (425 g).

FOR THE SALMON

Olive oil spray

4 (6-ounce/170 g) salmon fillets

Olive oil

Kosher salt and ground black pepper

1 large lime, sliced into 8 rounds

MAKES 4 SERVINGS

Prepare a grill over high heat.

To make the salsa, in a large bowl, combine the pineapple, serrano, onion, cilantro, lime juice, and salt and pepper to taste. Reserve about 1 cup (170 g) salsa for another use. (Serve it with chips for a late afternoon snack!)

To make the salmon, mist 4 sheets of aluminum foil with oil. Place a salmon fillet in the center of each sheet, drizzle with oil, and season with a few pinches of salt and pepper. Top each fillet with 2 slices of lime and one-fourth of the remaining salsa.

Fold the edges of the foil up and over the salmon and salsa to form a tight seal, leaving enough room for heat and steam to circulate inside the packets. Grill the packets for about 15 minutes, until the salmon is flaky and cooked through.

USE IT UP

There's no shortage of uses for a fresh bunch of cilantro. Use it up in Grilled Guacamole (page 106), Mexican Shrimp Cocktail (page 123), Mexican Street Corn Salad (page 122), Thai Quinoa Salad with a Trio of Fresh Herbs (page 75), Market-Fresh Taco Salad with Creamy Cilantro-Lime Dressing (page 80), Grilled Shrimp Tacos with Corn and Tomato Salsa (page 98), Red Lentil Soup with Carrot and Cumin (page 138), or Cuban Rice with Chicken (page 167).

(DON'T) FIRE IT UP!

Bacon has a lot of fat that can cause flare-ups on a grill, so keep a vigilant eye on your trout and move them around as needed to avoid fueling the fire. If using a charcoal grill, wait for the flames to taper off before placing the fish on the grate and cook them slightly away from the coals.

This camping staple is a classic for a reason. It's a foolproof recipe for the fresh catch of the day, you don't have to worry about the fish falling apart on the grill, and, well, who can say no to all that bacon? While trout is typically used, this recipe would work with other white fish as well, such as croaker, shad, sablefish, branzino, whiting, and perch. Kitchen twine helps hold the lemons and scallions together, but if it isn't something you usually remember to pack, tuck a case of unwaxed plain dental floss in your camping bin—it works in a pinch, and is great for slicing through soft cheeses too.

BACON-WRAPPED TROUT STUFFED WITH HERBS

MAKES 4 SERVINGS

4 (12- to 14-ounce/340 to 400 g) whole trout, butterflied and bones removed

Kosher salt and ground black pepper

Garlic powder

8 sprigs thyme

4 sprigs rosemary

2 large lemons, halved crosswise and sliced into thin half-moons

8 scallions

16 to 20 strips bacon

Prepare a grill over medium heat.

Season the trout inside and out with salt, pepper, and garlic powder. Stuff each trout with 2 sprigs thyme, 1 sprig rosemary, and a row of lemon slices. Layer one-fourth of the remaining lemon slices and 2 scallions on top. Wrap the trout with bacon, starting at the tail and tucking the end of the bacon strip under itself before continuing with another strip. You'll need 4 or 5 strips of bacon per fish. Tie a long length of kitchen twine around each trout to secure the fixings.

Grill the trout until a knife easily pierces the thickest part of the flesh and the bacon is crisp, 15 to 20 minutes, turning frequently to avoid flare-ups.

✧ USE IT UP ✧

If you find yourself with a few sprigs of thyme left, use them up in Savory Pancakes with Scallions, Mushrooms, and Goat Cheese (page 50), Grilled Watermelon with Gorgonzola and Pistachio Crumbles (page 133), or Dutch Oven Cider-Braised Pork Shoulder with Apple and Polenta (page 184). The rest of the rosemary can be used in Grilled Grape and Gorgonzola Pita Pizzas (page 92).

SMALL BITES

Trail snacks. Happy hour. Late-night nibbles. Morsels that get you through to the next meal. Little tastes of food aren't bound by time or place; they show up post-hike or pre-hammock, out on the coast or deep in the woods, and always at the right moment. Elevated by the sights and smells of the wild, this is food that's meant to be shared outside in good company.

Cooking avocado may not be the first thing you think to do with the fruit, but over a hot grill, the flesh turns smoky and savory, almost meaty in flavor. Just a few minutes on each side can elevate raw avocado into its own secret ingredient in this unconventional take on guac.

GRILLED GUACAMOLE

MAKES 2 CUPS (450 G)

3 small avocados, halved, pitted, and peeled

½ small red onion, root end left intact

1 medium tomato, finely chopped

Handful of cilantro leaves, chopped

½ jalapeño pepper, minced

2 cloves garlic, minced

¼ teaspoon kosher salt, plus more to taste

Juice of 1 medium lime

Prepare a grill over medium-high heat.

Place the avocados and onion cut sides down on the grill. Cook for about 10 minutes, until lightly charred with grill marks, turning once. Transfer to a cutting board. Cut the onion into small dice and cut the avocados into large chunks.

In a medium bowl, mash the avocado with a fork. Stir in the onion, tomato, cilantro, jalapeño, garlic, salt, and lime juice. Taste and add more salt as needed. Serve warm.

✦ USE IT UP ✦

Don't let that leftover cilantro get slimy. Use it up in Mexican Shrimp Cocktail (page 123), Mexican Street Corn Salad (page 122), Thai Quinoa Salad with a Trio of Fresh Herbs (page 75), Market-Fresh Taco Salad with Creamy Cilantro-Lime Dressing (page 80), Grilled Shrimp Tacos with Corn and Tomato Salsa (page 98), Foil-Pack Salmon with Pineapple Salsa (page 101), Red Lentil Soup with Carrot and Cumin (page 138), or Cuban Rice with Chicken (page 167).

This summertime salsa isn't just for chip-dippin'. The sweet and tangy combination of fruit also makes it suitable for topping yogurt and granola bowls, waffles, pancakes, crostini, and even pork chops and fish tacos. Use any of your favorite stone fruits in this recipe, including peaches, nectarines, apricots, plums, pluots, and cherries.

STONE FRUIT SALSA

MAKES 2 ½ CUPS (425 G)

1 pound (450 g) mixed stone fruits, pitted and finely diced

½ small red onion, finely diced

2 cloves garlic, minced

Handful of fresh basil leaves, chopped

Zest and juice of 1 medium lime

¼ teaspoon kosher salt, plus more to taste

Honey (optional)

Combine all of the ingredients in a large bowl. Taste and add more salt as needed. If desired, drizzle a little honey over the salsa before serving.

Nothing goes better with a cold one than these sophisticated beer nuts, which play-fully straddle the lines between salty and sweet, spicy and earthy. They're the type of nuts that usually make an appearance at holiday parties, but are just as enjoy-able year-round. I especially like them as "summit snacks"—small bites to share when you make it to the top at the end of the trail. If made ahead of time, the nuts store well in resealable plastic bags in a dry, cool place.

SPICED AND HERBED MIXED NUTS

MAKES 3 CUPS (435 G)

2 tablespoons olive oil

3 cups (435 g) unsalted mixed nuts

1 tablespoon kosher salt

1 tablespoon sugar

1 tablespoon chopped fresh rosemary

1 teaspoon chopped fresh thyme

¼ teaspoon ground cayenne pepper

Note: Any combination of nuts can be used in this recipe, but my favorites are cashews, almonds, walnuts, and pecans.

Heat the oil in a large skillet over medium-high heat. Add the nuts and stir to coat with oil. Cook until they deepen in color and turn fragrant, 3 to 5 minutes. Sprinkle the salt, sugar, rosemary, thyme, and cayenne pepper on top and stir to coat evenly. Let cool before serving.

✧ USE IT UP ✧

The fresh herbs can also be used in Savory Pancakes with Mushrooms, Scallions, and Goat Cheese (page 50), Grilled Watermelon with Gorgonzola and Pistachio Crumbles (page 133), Grilled Grape and Gorgonzola Pita Pizzas (page 92), Bacon-Wrapped Trout Stuffed with Herbs (page 103), Garlic-Herb Butter (page 161), or the herb-whipped goat cheese in Pile of Grilled Market Vegetables with Herbed Toasts (page 79).

TAKE YOUR TRAIL MIX
UP A NOTCH

Trail mix used to be a quick and simple snack for taking along on hikes. But these days, it's moved beyond basic GORP (good old raisins and peanuts) into a gourmet snack to tide you over on busy days and long drives. While premade trail mixes are widely available, it's more fun to make your own if you live near a store with a good bulk-foods aisle, such as Sprouts Farmers Market, WinCo Foods, or Whole Foods Market. Go ahead, get fancy with your mix!

Crystallized Ginger
Ginger is a natural remedy for easing altitude sickness and motion sickness, but sometimes it's a little hard to take on its own. The sugar coating on crystallized ginger nicely balances its spice, so it's a good ingredient to add if you're prone to nausea.

Seeds
If you're allergic to nuts or just want to shake things up a little, seeds pack a lot of protein in your trail mix. Try roasted watermelon seeds (a popular Asian snack found in many Chinese and Japanese markets) and pepitas (roasted hull-less pumpkin seeds).

Dried Fruits
Raisins and dried cranberries may be the de facto choices in the dried fruit department, but plenty of more interesting options exist. Try tart red cherries, goji berries, blueberries, figs, diced pineapple, banana chips, plantain chips, chile mango slices, or papaya slices.

Dried Legumes, Nuts, and Grains
Bring on the heat with wasabi peas and dry-roasted wasabi edamame, or explore seasoned varieties of nuts, like balsamic almonds, tamari almonds, and Cajun peanuts. Corn nuts add a salty, satisfying crunch, while the sweet and salty play of kettle corn makes it highly addictive.

Sweet Stuff
There are chocolates, and then there are things like chocolate-covered ginger, chocolate-covered espresso beans, chocolate-covered pretzels, malted milk balls, mini peanut butter cups, cocoa nibs, and nonpareils. You can also try yogurt-covered raisins, peanut brittle, and mini marshmallows. (Okay, so the marshmallows don't offer much by way of nutritional value . . . but sometimes, trail mix is really just a treat. So treat yourself!)

Known as dukkah, this warm aromatic blend of toasted nuts and seeds originated in Egypt. It has grown in popularity worldwide among chefs and food aficionados, who find varied uses for the versatile condiment. From sprinkling the dukkah over roasted vegetables to using it as a crust on pan-seared salmon, there are few things on which it isn't good. But my favorite way to enjoy it is also the traditional way: with pieces of flatbread dipped in olive oil before being dunked in dukkah. It's a simple snack, but so addictive!

EGYPTIAN NUT AND SPICE MIX

MAKES 1 CUP (110 G)

½ cup (73 g) unsalted mixed nuts

¼ cup (35 g) sesame seeds

2 tablespoons coriander seeds

1 tablespoon cumin seeds

1 teaspoon fennel seeds

1 teaspoon black peppercorns

1 teaspoon kosher salt

Good-quality extra-virgin olive oil

Crusty bread or flatbread, toasted or grilled

Note: Almost any of your favorite nuts will work in this recipe. Try hazelnuts, walnuts, peanuts, pine nuts, pecans, pistachios, cashews, almonds, or a combination. Dukkah is very much about personal taste and individual mixtures.

At Home

In a small skillet over medium heat, toast each of the nuts and seeds in separate batches for a few minutes until fragrant, shaking the skillet frequently for even toasting on all sides. Transfer to a wide, shallow dish and let cool.

Add all of the toasted nuts and seeds, peppercorns, and salt to a food processor and pulse until dry and crumbly. The mixture may be fine or coarse depending on personal preference, but check after every few pulses. You want to avoid overprocessing the ingredients, which will turn them into a paste. (Alternatively, you can use a mortar and pestle to pound the nuts and seeds into a coarse powder.)

Transfer the dukkah to an airtight container and store in a dry, cool place for up to 1 month. (Alternatively, you can refrigerate the dukkah to extend its shelf life.)

In Camp

Serve the dukkah with a small bowl of olive oil and a spread of grilled or toasted bread. Dip each piece of bread into the oil first, then into the dukkah.

This is the dish you bring to happy hour in camp when your crew is pouring respectable bottles of wine and whiskey but passing uninspired handfuls of trail mix. You might be drinking out of enamelware mugs, but you can pretend you're at a sultry tapas bar with these plump, delectable dates. A single bite into an unassuming nugget yields a surprising variety of tastes and textures all at once, from sweet to savory, soft to crunchy. Serve them on their own or along with some cheese.

BACON-WRAPPED DATES

MAKES 16 DATES

16 Medjool dates, pitted (see Note)

¼ cup (36 g) almonds

8 strips bacon, cut in half

Note: Medjool dates can be found in the produce department of most well-stocked supermarkets. Look for large, plump dates with slightly glossy skins.

Stuff each date with 2 or 3 almonds, then wrap a slice of bacon around the date.

Heat a large skillet over medium-high heat. Arrange the dates in a single layer with the bacon seams facing down. Cook until the bacon is browned and crisp all over, 8 to 10 minutes, turning occasionally.

Transfer the dates to paper towel–lined plates to drain. Pierce each date with a toothpick for serving.

Make a Meze

If your idea of a great meal is lots of little nibbles rather than one large dish, put meze on the menu. The word *meze* means "taste" or "little snack," and it's a collection of small plates that features prominently in Eastern Mediterranean, Middle Eastern, and Arab cuisine. Like its Spanish cousin, tapas, meze is meant to be shared at the table in the company of good friends and good wine.

While Americans might consider meze to be a first course, it's more than just appetizers; it's a meal in its own right. You can easily assemble a meze spread in camp with a mix of homemade and store-bought finger foods, and make it a simple leisurely lunch or a hassle-free first night's meal.

Try a few of these small bites for building your own meze spread. Most are easy to make or easy to find in well-stocked supermarkets and delis.

- Bacon-Wrapped Dates (page 114)

- Egyptian Nut and Spice Mix (page 112)

- Naan, pita, or other flatbread (page 94)

- Good-quality olive oil

- Hummus

- Baba ghanoush

- Tapenade

- Dolmas (stuffed grape leaves)

- Kalamata and green olives

- Persian or English cucumbers, sliced

- Cherry tomatoes

- Sun-dried tomatoes

- Marinated artichoke hearts

- Marinated roasted red bell peppers, sliced

- Peppadew peppers

- Roasted garlic

- Halloumi cheese, sliced and grilled

- Block of feta cheese, cubed and drizzled with olive oil

- Labneh (Lebanese strained yogurt)

- Greek yogurt

- Tzatziki

- Cured meats

- Fresh fruit

Quick and easy crostini ("little toasts" in Italian) can be served as an afternoon snack or as a first course to dinner. The thin slices of bread are merely a vehicle for an array of creative toppings, whether your tastes run sweet (perhaps Greek yogurt with honey-drizzled berries?) or savory (try pimento cheese with bacon, or goat cheese with olive tapenade). The two variations here make the most of seasonal summer fruit and bring sweet and savory together when you just can't decide. If you live near an Italian or specialty market, try to find freshly made ricotta—the flavor and texture blows away the supermarket stuff.

CAMP CROSTINI

Fig, Salami, and Ricotta Crostini

MAKES 12 CROSTINI

12 thin slices French baguette

1½ cups (340 g) ricotta cheese

12 thin slices Genoa salami

4 medium figs, cut into eighths

Balsamic vinegar

Freshly cracked black pepper (optional)

In a large skillet over medium-high heat, toast the bread until crisp and golden brown on both sides, 2 to 4 minutes, turning once.

Top each slice of toast with 2 tablespoons of ricotta, 1 slice of salami, 2 or 3 slices of fig, and a drizzle of balsamic. If desired, finish with freshly cracked black pepper.

Peach, Prosciutto, and Ricotta Crostini

MAKES 12 CROSTINI

12 thin slices French baguette

4 thin slices prosciutto

1½ cups (340 g) ricotta cheese

1 large peach, pitted and thinly sliced

Honey

Freshly cracked black pepper (optional)

In a large skillet over medium-high heat, toast the bread until crisp and golden brown on both sides, 2 to 4 minutes, turning once.

Tear the prosciutto into feathery slivers. Top each slice of toast with 2 tablespoons of ricotta, a few pieces of prosciutto, 1 or 2 slices of peach, and a drizzle of honey. If desired, finish with freshly cracked black pepper.

When I close my eyes and think about that first bite of smoky, steamy charred corn straight off the grill, slathered generously with butter, I'm immediately taken back to long, lazy, leisurely days in my happy place, whether it's in the mountains, on a lake, or by a river. No summer camping trip feels complete without a few fresh cobs cooking over a fire. And while you can't go wrong with butter, you can go so right with these other ideas for toppings.

GRILLED CORN ON THE COB, 4 WAYS

MAKES 4 SERVINGS

FOR THE CORN

4 ears corn, shucked

Prepare a grill over high heat.

Place the corn on the grill and cook until just tender and charred on all sides, 6 to 8 minutes, rotating the cobs every 2 minutes. Dress with one of the toppings below.

Mexican Street Style

½ cup (113 g) mayonnaise

½ cup (56 g) crumbled Cotija cheese

2 tablespoons chile powder

1 lime, cut into wedges

Slather each cob with a heaping spoonful of mayonnaise, followed by a generous sprinkle of Cotija and a light dusting of chile powder. Squeeze a wedge of lime over each cob before serving.

Garlicky Parmesan

½ cup (113 g) butter, softened

2 tablespoons chopped fresh parsley leaves

½ teaspoon garlic powder

½ cup (50 g) grated Parmesan cheese

In a small bowl, stir together the butter, parsley, and garlic powder until well combined. Thickly slather the butter on each cob, followed by a generous sprinkle of Parmesan.

Dilly Horseradish

½ cup (113 g) mayonnaise

2 tablespoons chopped
fresh dill

2 tablespoons prepared
horseradish

In a small bowl, stir together all of the ingredients until
well combined. Slather each cob liberally with the
mayonnaise mixture.

Zesty Cilantro

½ cup (113 g) butter,
softened

2 tablespoons chopped
cilantro leaves

¼ teaspoon ground
cayenne pepper

Juice of 1 medium lime

In a small bowl, stir together the butter, cilantro, cayenne
pepper, and lime juice until well combined. Liberally
slather the butter mixture on each cob.

If you lack a grill to make elotes (otherwise known as Mexican street corn, page 120), meet its cousin, esquites (or Mexican street corn salad). It's essentially a deconstructed version, and you'll find all the usual players: the chile-flecked corn, the creamy mayo (or crema Mexicana), the crumbly Cotija, and a tangy squeeze of lime. But in this stovetop recipe, the kernels get their characteristic char from a blistering pan, which infuses the salad with even more flavor. It's a satisfying snack as well as a steak-friendly side dish (with the added perk of not having to pick corn out of your teeth afterward!).

MEXICAN STREET CORN SALAD

MAKES 4 SERVINGS

2 tablespoons sunflower oil

4 ears corn, shucked and kernels removed

½ teaspoon kosher salt

⅓ cup (37 g) crumbled Cotija cheese

⅓ cup (20 g) thinly sliced scallion

⅓ cup (16 g) chopped cilantro

2 tablespoons mayonnaise or crema Mexicana

1 teaspoon chile powder

1 jalapeño pepper, minced

2 cloves garlic, minced

Juice of 1 medium lime

Heat a large skillet over medium-high heat and swirl in the oil. Add the corn kernels and salt and cook undisturbed until the kernels are charred on the bottom, 2 to 3 minutes. Stir them around and cook undisturbed until the kernels are charred on the other side, 2 to 3 minutes. Stir again and cook until most of the kernels are charred all over, about 5 minutes more. Remove the skillet from the heat.

In a large bowl, stir together the Cotija cheese, scallion, cilantro, mayonnaise, chile powder, jalapeño, garlic, and lime juice. Add the corn and toss to combine. Serve warm.

✧ USE IT UP ✧

Cilantro adds flair to so many recipes. Use it up in Grilled Guacamole (page 106), Mexican Shrimp Cocktail (page 123), Thai Quinoa Salad with a Trio of Fresh Herbs (page 75), Market-Fresh Taco Salad with Creamy Cilantro-Lime Dressing (page 80), Grilled Shrimp Tacos with Corn and Tomato Salsa (page 98), Foil-Pack Salmon with Pineapple Salsa (page 101), Red Lentil Soup with Carrot and Cumin (page 138), or Cuban Rice with Chicken (page 167).

On a sweltering summer day, this cold and refreshing, spicy and zesty shrimp cocktail totally hits the spot. Serve it up in a mug to make a portable nibble you can bring with you as you plant your chair on the riverbank, sink your feet into the rushing water, and soak up the afternoon sun. Add a Paloma (page 193) or 3-2-1 Margarita (page 193) to the mix and life is good, my friend. Really good.

MEXICAN SHRIMP COCKTAIL

MAKES 4 SERVINGS

1½ cups (350 ml) tomato and clam juice cocktail, chilled (see Note)

½ cup (120 g) ketchup, chilled

Juice of 2 medium limes

2 tablespoons Mexican hot sauce

½ teaspoon kosher salt

¼ teaspoon ground black pepper

1 pound (450 g) cooked large shrimp, peeled and deveined (16/20 count)

2 medium tomatoes, diced

1 medium English cucumber, diced (about ½ pound)

½ small red onion, diced

1 jalapeño pepper, minced

⅓ cup (16 g) chopped cilantro leaves

1 small avocado, pitted, peeled, and sliced

1 medium lime, cut into wedges

Note: Tomato and clam juice cocktail (also called Clamato) can be found in the juice aisle of well-stocked supermarkets.

In a large bowl, combine the tomato and clam juice cocktail, ketchup, lime juice, hot sauce, salt, and pepper. Taste and add more hot sauce, salt, and pepper as desired.

Stir in the shrimp, tomatoes, cucumber, onion, jalapeño, and cilantro. Cover and chill for at least 1 hour for the flavors to develop. Serve with a few slices of avocado on top and lime wedges on the side.

✧ USE IT UP ✧

There's no shortage of uses for a fresh bunch of cilantro. Use it up in Grilled Guacamole (page 106), Mexican Street Corn Salad (page 122), Thai Quinoa Salad with a Trio of Fresh Herbs (page 75), Market-Fresh Taco Salad with Creamy Cilantro-Lime Dressing (page 80), Grilled Shrimp Tacos with Corn and Tomato Salsa (page 98), Foil-Pack Salmon with Pineapple Salsa (page 101), Red Lentil Soup with Carrot and Cumin (page 138), or Cuban Rice with Chicken (page 167).

The pizza "crust" in this recipe is ready-made polenta, typically found packaged in a tube. It's one of my favorite shortcuts in camp, since it beats stirring a pot of cornmeal on the stove until it turns into porridge. Unlike polenta made from scratch, prepared polenta starts out firm, which works to our advantage here. By frying the polenta in a pan, the base of these mini margherita pizzas get just the right amount of crispy on the bottom while staying soft and chewy on the inside. They're filling without giving you that too-full feeling!

MARGHERITA POLENTA PIZZA BITES

MAKES 12 PIZZA BITES

1 (18-ounce/510 g) tube prepared polenta, sliced into 12 rounds

2 tablespoons olive oil

¾ cup (180 ml) No-Cook Pizza Sauce (page 147) or store-bought pizza sauce

8 ounces (226 g) fresh mozzarella, sliced into 12 rounds

12 fresh basil leaves

2 large plum tomatoes, sliced into 12 rounds and drained

Red pepper flakes (optional)

Spread the polenta rounds on paper towels to drain excess moisture for about 15 minutes, then pat dry with more towels.

Heat a large skillet over medium-high heat. Add the oil and swirl it around to coat the surface. Arrange the polenta rounds in a single layer and cook undisturbed until the edges begin to crisp and the bottoms are golden brown, 6 to 8 minutes.

Flip the polenta and top each polenta round with 1 tablespoon sauce, 1 mozzarella slice, 1 basil leaf, and 1 tomato slice. Cover and cook until the cheese is melted, 3 to 5 minutes.

Serve with a sprinkle of red pepper flakes, if desired.

 **MIX IT UP**

Try other toppings on the polenta crusts, such as pesto, barbecue sauce, pepperoni, olives, scallions, fresh or marinated bell peppers, artichoke hearts, cooked chicken, and shredded Cheddar.

Think of this as the lighter cousin of Caesar but with more depth of flavor. Flame-licked lettuce, char-grilled lemons, and garlic-smashed anchovies come together in a bright, bold salad that doesn't want to stay on the sidelines. To ensure the leaves will actually sear on the grill and not simply steam, rinse and dry them well. You want as little moisture on the leaves as possible so they'll retain their crispness while soaking up all the smokiness from the grill.

CHARRED ROMAINE SALAD WITH LEMON-ANCHOVY DRESSING

MAKES 4 SERVINGS

6 oil-packed anchovy fillets, drained and finely chopped

2 cloves garlic, minced

1 teaspoon Dijon mustard

½ teaspoon red pepper flakes

3 large hearts romaine lettuce, halved lengthwise (about 1 pound/450 g)

2 medium lemons, halved crosswise

½ cup (120 ml) olive oil, plus more for drizzling

Grated Parmesan cheese

Prepare a grill over high heat.

In a small bowl, mash the anchovies, garlic, mustard, and red pepper flakes together and set aside.

Drizzle the lettuce with a little oil and grill, cut sides down, until charred with good grill marks, 2 to 3 minutes. Flip and grill the other side until the outer leaves are slightly wilted and browned on the edges, about 2 minutes. Grill the lemon halves, cut sides down, for 2 to 3 minutes, until the bottoms are charred.

Juice the lemons into the bowl of anchovies. Whisk in the oil until well combined.

Transfer the lettuce to a cutting board and coarsely chop the leaves. Divide among 4 plates, drizzle with the dressing, and top with a sprinkle of Parmesan.

Cabbage on its own is a humble vegetable, but sear it on the grill and it can be the star of a dish. The leaves become just a touch more tender without losing their crispness, and the sharp, creamy dressing marries beautifully with the smoky bits of char. Green and red cabbage can be used interchangeably in this recipe, and they make an especially pretty slaw when combined. Or be bold and try a head of radicchio—the tangy dressing will temper its bitterness.

GRILLED COLESLAW WITH CREAMY GORGONZOLA VINAIGRETTE

MAKES 4 SERVINGS

½ cup (113 g) mayonnaise

½ cup (113 g) sour cream

½ cup (56 g) crumbled Gorgonzola cheese

2 tablespoons white vinegar

½ teaspoon kosher salt

½ teaspoon ground black pepper

1 small head cabbage, cut into 8 wedges, core left intact (about 1½ pounds/680 g)

Olive oil spray

1 medium lemon, halved crosswise

Prepare a grill over high heat.

In a small bowl, stir together the mayonnaise, sour cream, Gorgonzola, vinegar, salt, and pepper until well combined.

Spray the cut sides of the cabbage with oil and grill for 4 to 5 minutes on each cut side (total of 8 to 10 minutes), until the edges of the leaves are charred. The cabbage should be slightly wilted but still crunchy in the center. Grill the lemon halves, cut sides down, for 2 to 3 minutes, until the bottoms are charred.

Juice the lemons into the bowl of vinaigrette and stir to combine. Serve the cabbage wedges whole or finely chopped with a drizzle of vinaigrette on top.

✧ MIX IT UP ✧

For added color, texture, and flavor, try thinly sliced radish, grated carrot, or grilled scallions in the slaw.

This fruity spin on the classic Caprese salad marries peak-of-summer peaches with juicy tomatoes, fresh mozzarella, and fragrant balsamic—a succulent union that sweetens up all those heavy, smoky meats coming off the campfire grill. Use the most beautiful and colorful heirloom tomatoes you can find for a vivid presentation.

PEAK-OF-SUMMER PEACH CAPRESE SALAD

MAKES 4 SERVINGS

1 large peach, pitted and cut into ¾-inch (2-cm) slices

2 medium tomatoes, cut into ¾-inch (2-cm) slices

4 ounces (113 g) fresh mozzarella, cut into half-moons

Handful of fresh basil leaves

Olive oil

Balsamic vinegar

Kosher salt and ground black pepper

On a serving dish, arrange the salad by alternating the peaches, tomatoes, and mozzarella in rows. Tuck the basil between the fruit and cheese. Drizzle generously with oil and vinegar, aiming for a ratio of 2:1 oil to vinegar. Top the salad with a sprinkle of salt and pepper to taste.

✦ MIX IT UP ✦

For deeper and sweeter flavor, grill the peaches over medium heat for 2 minutes on each side until lightly charred and caramelized.

Outside of Mexican cuisine, crisp, airy tomatillos are somewhat of a mystery compared to their juicy, squishy sibling, tomatoes. Most people have had tomatillos simmered, roasted, or broiled in salsa, carnitas, or chile verde, but few recipes exist for raw, fresh tomatillos. In this recipe, however, their slightly sour, almost citrusy and kiwi-like flavor is the star of the salad. It just might convince you to try tomatillos in their natural state if you haven't yet.

TANGY TOMATILLO, TOMATO, AND STRAWBERRY SALAD

MAKES 4 SERVINGS

4 medium tomatillos, husked and cut into ¼-inch (6-mm) wedges

1½ cups (225 g) halved cherry tomatoes

1½ cups (250 g) hulled and halved strawberries

⅓ cup (56 g) oil-packed sun-dried tomatoes, drained and chopped

1 serrano pepper, minced

2 tablespoons olive oil

1 tablespoon balsamic vinegar

Kosher salt and ground black pepper

In a large bowl, combine the tomatillos, cherry tomatoes, strawberries, sun-dried tomatoes, and serrano pepper.

Whisk together the oil and vinegar in a small bowl, then pour over the salad and toss to coat. Season with salt and pepper to taste.

MORE SWEET AND SAVORY SUGGESTIONS

Strange as it sounds, watermelon and cheese are a winning duo on and off the grill. For another classic combination, toss cubed watermelon with crumbled feta and mint, or substitute watermelon for tomato in a Caprese salad.

Try a dollop of goat cheese on grilled watermelon with slivers of pickled red onions, or serve the wedges hot off the grill with a smear of mascarpone and a squeeze of lemon.

In Cyprus, watermelon is often paired with halloumi as a summertime snack, and it just so happens that one of the best ways to prepare halloumi, a semi-hard cheese, is to grill it. In fact, it is sometimes called grilling cheese because of its high melting point, allowing it to brown before it melts.

For an unexpected but delicious hors d'oeuvres, top watermelon wedges with Gruyère or fontina and stick them under the broiler for a few minutes. Finish with a sprinkle of your favorite herbs before serving.

A heaping pile of watermelon served on a hot summer day is a good thing. Grilling the watermelon takes it to great. But how do you make a great thing even better? By topping it with a handful of crumbly Gorgonzola and crunchy pistachios, a combination that somehow just works when the watermelon is slightly caramelized from the heat of a grill. If you grow your own thyme at home or frequent farmers' markets, try lemon thyme in this recipe. The hint of citrus brightens the smoky sweetness of the fruit.

GRILLED WATERMELON WITH GORGONZOLA AND PISTACHIO CRUMBLES

MAKES 4 TO 6 SERVINGS

1 (5-pound/2.2-kg) seedless baby watermelon, cut into 1-inch-thick wedges

Crumbled Gorgonzola cheese

Chopped pistachios

Chopped fresh thyme

Prepare a grill over medium-high heat.

Place the watermelon on the grill and cook for 2 to 3 minutes on each side, until the surface is seared and glossy but the interior retains its crunch. Sprinkle with a few handfuls of Gorgonzola, pistachios, and thyme to taste.

 USE IT UP

Don't throw out the rest of that thyme! Use it up in Savory Pancakes with Scallions, Mushrooms, and Goat Cheese (page 51), Bacon-Wrapped Trout Stuffed with Herbs (page 103), or Dutch Oven Cider-Braised Pork Shoulder with Apple and Polenta (page 32).

CAMP
FEASTS

As the sun sets over the trees, the alpenglow fades from the peaks and
the sky starts to sparkle with a billion brilliant gems, the first
wisps of smoke are seen rising from camp. Friends and
family pull up their seats and gather around a
crackling campfire. Laughter echoes through
the woods, bottles of wine are poured
into enamelware mugs, and
the savory smell of good
food fills the air.
Tonight, we
feast.

FOR THE SAUCE

1 tablespoon olive oil

½ medium yellow onion, chopped

4 cloves garlic, minced

5 medium tomatoes, chopped (about 2 pounds/900 g; see Note)

¼ cup (56 g) butter

2 teaspoons dried Italian seasoning

½ teaspoon kosher salt

Note: Don't want to deal with fresh tomatoes at camp? Substitute a 28-ounce (800 g) can of diced tomatoes for the fresh.

FOR THE SKEWERS

3 medium zucchini, cut into ½-inch (1-cm) slices (about 1½ pounds/680 g)

3 medium yellow summer squash, cut into ½-inch (1-cm) slices (about 1½ pounds/680 g)

2 medium Chinese eggplant, cut into ½-inch (1-cm) slices (about 1 pound/450 g; see Note)

Olive oil spray

Kosher salt and ground black pepper

Note: Chinese eggplant is a thin-skinned, long and slender version of the vegetable found in most Asian and specialty markets. If you aren't able to source it, substitute Japanese eggplant or slice a conventional eggplant to size.

A rugged take on the classic French Provençal stew, these ratatouille skewers are pretty to look at and fun to make. You can even involve the kids for the task of "kebabing" them in the camp kitchen! The key to grilling all the vegetables evenly—and making them look good—is ensuring they're more or less the same girth. If you can't find suitable summer squash, try golden zucchini, which tends to be more uniform in shape.

GRILLED RATATOUILLE SKEWERS

MAKES 4 SERVINGS

To make the sauce, heat a small saucepan over medium-high heat. Swirl in the oil, then add the onion and garlic and cook until the onion starts to turn translucent, 2 to 3 minutes. Stir in the tomatoes, butter, Italian seasoning, and salt. Simmer, stirring occasionally, until the sauce is done.

Prepare a grill for medium-high heat.

To make the skewers, thread the zucchini, yellow summer squash, and eggplant onto 4 skewers, alternating the colors. Lightly spray the vegetables with oil and season with salt and pepper. Grill the skewers for about 20 minutes, turning frequently so all sides cook evenly.

Pour the tomato sauce over the vegetables before serving.

✧ MIX IT UP ✧

Serve the ratatouille and tomato sauce with grilled bread or over pasta. Leftover vegetables can be served cold over salad greens. Any remaining tomato sauce can be spooned over the next morning's omelet or egg scramble.

Soup and cold weather go hand in hand. It's the type of meal you make when it's early spring, the first camping trip of the year, and you can see your own breath while huddled over the stove with your headlamp. This wholesome and warming soup is exactly what you need after a long day of exploring, and it comes together in no time at all, since red lentils cook faster than their green and brown counterparts.

RED LENTIL SOUP WITH CARROT AND CUMIN

MAKES 4 SERVINGS

2 tablespoons olive oil

1 medium yellow onion, chopped

3 cloves garlic, minced

2 medium carrots, diced

1 rib celery, diced

1 tablespoon tomato paste

1 teaspoon ground cumin

¼ teaspoon ground cayenne pepper

1 cup (192 g) dried red lentils

5 cups (12 dL) chicken broth

Juice of 1 lemon

Handful of cilantro leaves, chopped

In a stockpot over medium-high heat, drizzle the oil. Add the onion and garlic and cook until the onion starts to turn translucent, 2 to 3 minutes. Add the carrots, celery, tomato paste, cumin, and cayenne and cook for about 5 minutes, until the vegetables are crisp-tender and thoroughly coated, stirring occasionally. Add the lentils and broth and bring to a boil.

Reduce the heat, cover, and simmer for 15 to 20 minutes, until the lentils are soft. Stir in the lemon juice and garnish with cilantro before serving.

✧ USE IT UP ✧

Stuck with a whole can of tomato paste and don't want to bring it back home? Use it up in One-Pot Penne alla Vodka (page 178), Five-Alarm Three-Bean Chili (page 142), or Dutch Oven Old-School Lasagna (page 179). Cilantro's right at home in Grilled Guacamole (page 106), Mexican Shrimp Cocktail (page 123), Mexican Street Corn Salad (page 122), Thai Quinoa Salad with a Trio of Fresh Herbs (page 75), Market-Fresh Taco Salad with Creamy Cilantro-Lime Dressing (page 80), Grilled Shrimp Tacos with Corn and Tomato Salsa (page 98), or Cuban Rice with Chicken (page 167).

I love the simplicity of a good peasant stew. When the sky turns gray and the threat of rain looms over camp, I turn to a meal like this: a wholesome, hearty, warming one-pot meal that's ready by the time the first raindrops fall and the chairs are moved under the vestibule. I've made countless variations of this stew for years, sometimes adding sausage or potato, or kale instead of chard, but three things always stay the same: a flavor base of mirepoix, a few handfuls of fresh greens, and a good amount of creamy cannellini beans, lightly mashed to make a thicker broth.

TUSCAN BEANS AND GREENS STEW

MAKES 4 SERVINGS

2 tablespoons olive oil

1 medium yellow onion, chopped

3 cloves garlic, minced

2 medium carrots, diced

1 rib celery, diced

2 teaspoons dried Italian seasoning

½ teaspoon red pepper flakes

3 cups (700 ml) chicken broth

2 (15-ounce/425 g) cans cannellini beans, rinsed and drained (see Note)

1 (14-ounce/400 g) can diced tomatoes

3 cups (110 g) chopped chard

Grated Parmesan cheese

In a stockpot over medium-high heat, drizzle the oil. Add the onion and garlic and cook until the onion starts to turn translucent, 2 to 3 minutes. Add the carrots, celery, Italian seasoning, and red pepper flakes and cook until the vegetables are tender, about 5 minutes, stirring occasionally. Pour in the broth, beans, and tomatoes and bring to a boil.

Lightly mash one-third of the beans with a large spoon. Stir in the chard, reduce the heat, and simmer for 10 to 15 minutes, until the chard is soft and the stew is thickened.

Serve with a sprinkle of Parmesan on top.

Note: Though this recipe calls for canned cannellini beans, any white bean will work, including Great Northern beans or navy beans.

Like other stews in the Spanish region, this Catalan recipe starts with sofrito, a thick sauce of onion, pepper, and tomato that gives the broth its rich aroma (and sets the foundation for other Latin recipes, like Cuban Rice with Chicken on page 167). It's the perfect thing to put on the stove when temperatures start dropping and a hearty, steamy bowl of stew is exactly what you need to warm your hands and sate that post-hike hunger.

SPANISH CHORIZO AND CHICKPEA STEW

MAKES 4 TO 6 SERVINGS

¼ cup (60 ml) olive oil

4 cloves garlic, minced

1 medium yellow onion, chopped

1 medium bell pepper, cored and chopped

1 bay leaf

½ teaspoon dried thyme

½ teaspoon kosher salt

1 (28-ounce/800 g) can crushed tomatoes

3 (15-ounce/425 g) cans chickpeas, rinsed and drained

3 links soft Spanish chorizo, thinly sliced (about 8 ounces/226 g; see Note)

2 cups (475 ml) chicken broth

3 cups (100 g) packed baby spinach

Ground black pepper

In a stockpot, heat the oil over medium-high heat. Add the garlic and cook until lightly browned, 1 to 2 minutes. Add the onion, bell pepper, bay leaf, thyme, and salt and cook until the onion is soft and translucent and the pepper is tender, about 5 minutes. Pour in the tomatoes and simmer for 5 minutes to let the flavors intermingle. Add the chickpeas, chorizo, and broth and bring to a boil, stirring occasionally.

Reduce the heat and simmer for about 15 minutes, until the stew is thickened. Stir in the spinach and cook until just wilted. Season with pepper to taste.

Note: There are two types of Spanish chorizo, soft and hard, and this recipe calls for the soft, semi-cured chorizo sold in short links (sometimes called cooking chorizo). Hard, dry-cured chorizo, sold as longer, thinner loops or thicker rolls, are typically sliced and used for cold cuts. Both are denser in texture and different in flavor from Mexican chorizo, which is a fresh (raw) crumbly sausage. Fresh chorizo is not a suitable substitute for semi-cured, though dry chorizo can be used if this is all you can find. Look for Spanish chorizo in better supermarkets and specialty markets.

1 tablespoon olive oil

1 medium yellow onion, chopped

3 cloves garlic, minced

1 medium bell pepper, cored and diced

1 poblano pepper, minced

1 Anaheim pepper, minced

1 jalapeño pepper, minced

2 canned chipotle chiles in adobo sauce, minced, plus 2 tablespoons sauce

2 tablespoons tomato paste

1 tablespoon sugar

1 teaspoon ground cumin

1 teaspoon dried oregano

1 (28-ounce/800 g) can crushed tomatoes

2 cups chicken broth

1 (12-ounce/350 ml) bottle beer

1 (15-ounce/425 g) can kidney beans, rinsed and drained

1 (15-ounce/425 g) can black beans, rinsed and drained

1 (15-ounce/425 g) can pinto beans, rinsed and drained

Sour cream

Shredded sharp Cheddar cheese

Sliced scallions

While some might argue that chili isn't chili without meat (or with beans, for that matter), this three-bean stew is far from lacking in flavor. Five types of peppers, ranging from sweet to smoky to spicy, give a complexity in flavor that you just can't get from chili powder alone. I don't specify a particular beer in this recipe, but some type of beer is essential for a multilayered broth and the one you choose will become your secret ingredient. I'm partial to stouts (especially the more intriguing ones like chocolate or coffee stouts) for their deep maltiness and to red ales for the touch of sweetness they bring to all the spice. However, if you prefer pale ales, pour your favorite into the pot; the hoppy bitterness enhances the heat of the peppers.

FIVE-ALARM THREE-BEAN CHILI

MAKES 6 SERVINGS

In a stockpot over medium-high heat, swirl in the oil. Add the onion and garlic and cook until the onion starts to turn translucent, 2 to 3 minutes. Stir in all of the peppers, adobo sauce, tomato paste, sugar, cumin, and oregano and cook until the peppers are crisp-tender and the mixture is fragrant, about 5 minutes. Pour in the tomatoes, broth, and beer and bring to a boil.

Reduce the heat and simmer for 20 minutes, stirring occasionally. Add all of the beans and continue simmering for 10 minutes more until the beans are heated through.

Serve with a dollop of sour cream and a handful of cheese and scallions on top.

✧ USE IT UP ✧

Tomato paste is one of those things you usually forget about after you've used it once, so use up the rest of it in Red Lentil Soup with Carrot and Cumin (page 138), One-Pot Penne alla Vodka (page 178), or Dutch Oven Old-School Lasagna (page 179).

No grill? No oven? No problem. Homemade pizza can still be had at the convenience of your camp stove. The key to this and all other pizza recipes in the book is mise en place—that is, having everything in place before you begin to top the pizza. The tomatoes should be sliced, the prosciutto torn, the corn shucked, and the cheese shredded so that your pie is ready for assembly as soon as you flip the dough in the pan. This allows you to work quickly, keeps the kitchen tidy, and saves the dough from scorching. A cast-iron pan is preferable for its heat-retaining qualities, but any heavy-bottom 12-inch skillet will work for this recipe.

STOVETOP SKILLET PIZZA WITH FRESH CORN, TOMATO, PROSCIUTTO, AND PESTO

MAKES 4 SERVINGS

1 pound (450 g) Homemade Pizza Dough (page 146) or store-bought pizza dough

Olive oil spray

⅔ cup (150 g) store-bought pesto

2 medium tomatoes, sliced (about ½ pound/226 g)

2 thin slices prosciutto, torn into slivers

1 ear corn, shucked and kernels removed

½ cup (56 g) shredded mozzarella cheese

4 ounces (113 g) goat cheese, cut into small pieces

Bring the chilled pizza dough to room temperature for about 30 minutes.

Heat a large skillet over medium-high heat and lightly spray the surface with oil. Divide the dough in half and shape into 2 smooth balls. Working with the first ball of dough, flatten and stretch it into a 10-inch (25-cm) round. Place the dough in the skillet and cook until bubbles begin to form on the surface and the bottom is golden brown, 1 to 2 minutes. Lightly spray the top of the crust with oil and turn it over.

RECIPE CONTINUES

TOOL TIP

If you have trouble stretching the dough by hand, place the ball of dough on a lightly oiled sheet of aluminum foil and flatten the dough slightly. Lay another oiled sheet of foil on top (with the oiled side facing down) and use the side of a wine bottle or Nalgene bottle to roll out the dough.

Working quickly, spread half the pesto evenly over the crust, followed by half each of the tomatoes, prosciutto, corn, mozzarella, and goat cheese. Reduce the heat to medium, cover, and cook until the bottom is crisp and browned, the mozzarella is melted, and all the ingredients are warmed through, 3 to 5 minutes. If the bottom is browning rapidly but the cheese isn't melted yet, reduce the heat further to prevent the crust from burning.

Repeat the process to make the second pizza.

 ✦ MIX IT UP ✦

The secret to a successful skillet pizza (and grilled pizza, page 148) is making sure your toppings are fully cooked or do not need to be cooked before adding them. Sauté, steam, or grill them ahead of time, as the residual heat from the stove or grill only serves to melt the cheese and warm the toppings. That said, good choices for toppings include pepperoni (of course!), leftover cooked steak or chicken, sun-dried tomatoes, sautéed onions, sautéed mushrooms, grilled summer squash, raw spinach, raw avocado, raw bell peppers, marinated roasted red bell peppers, and marinated artichoke hearts.

Homemade Pizza Dough

Put down that premade crust—homemade pizza in camp is less work than you think. This easy, everyday pizza dough has the right amount of chewiness and crispness, whether you're in the mood for thin crust, deep dish, or anything in between. It cooks just as well in an oven—even a dutch oven—as it does in a skillet or grill, making it the only pizza dough recipe you'll ever need. It also freezes well and travels well, so make a double or triple batch to keep at home and bring to camp.

This recipe can be used for pizza (pages 143, 149, and 177) and flatbread (page 94), as well as breadsticks and calzones.

MAKES 1 POUND

1 cup (240 ml) warm water (100°F to 110°F)

1 teaspoon active dry yeast

1 teaspoon sugar

1 teaspoon kosher salt

2 tablespoons olive oil, plus more for greasing

2½ cups (300 g) all-purpose flour

Note: If you frequently make personal-size pizzas, divide the dough into 2 (½-pound/226 g) balls before freezing for added convenience.

Lightly grease a medium bowl and set aside.

In another medium bowl, add the water, yeast, sugar, and salt and stir with a large sturdy spoon to combine (the ingredients do not need to be dissolved). Add the oil and flour and mix until no dry pockets remain and a shaggy dough forms.

Knead the dough by hand for 3 to 5 minutes, until it looks and feels smooth. Shape the dough into a ball and lightly coat with oil. Place it in the greased bowl and cover with plastic wrap. Let rise at room temperature for 1 to 1½ hours, until it has doubled in volume.

Remove the dough from the bowl, smooth it into a ball, and tightly wrap it in plastic wrap. Chill for up to 3 days, or for longer term storage, place the dough in a freezer bag and freeze for up to 1 month. Thaw the dough overnight in the refrigerator (or cooler) before using.

No-Cook Pizza Sauce

Many recipes for pizza sauce require you to cook it down on the stove, but not cooking it is the secret ingredient in this homemade sauce. By giving everything a whirl in the blender and storing it in the fridge, you retain all the freshness and flavor of juicy, ripe tomatoes that carries over into the pizza. Use this sauce with Grilled Pizza Primavera (page 149), Dutch Oven Deep-Dish Soppressata and Fennel Pizza (page 177), or your favorite pizza concoction.

MAKES 2 TO 2½ CUPS (475 TO 585 ML)

4 medium plum tomatoes, quartered (about 1 pound/450 g)

1 (6-ounce/170 g) can tomato paste

4 cloves garlic

2 tablespoons olive oil

2 teaspoons dried Italian seasoning

1 teaspoon sugar

1 teaspoon kosher salt

1 teaspoon ground black pepper

Add all of the ingredients to a blender or food processor. Blend or process until smooth. Transfer the sauce to a lidded container and chill for up to 1 week. The sauce can also be frozen for up to 3 months.

✦ NO LEAKS LEFT BEHIND ✦

My favorite way to transport liquid food items is in food-grade wide-mouth Nalgene bottles. The BPA-free plastic bottles are leak-proof and able to take a lot of abuse in camp, whether you cram them into a cooler or drop them on a boulder. They're ideal for storing sauces, marinades, broths, and soups, and they also double as ice packs if you freeze them ahead of your camping trip.

Like the pasta that inspired it, this pizza primavera is loaded with fresh spring vegetables. When the veggies are picked at their peak and eaten in season, little more is needed to enhance their sweetness than the kiss of a grill. This is the kind of pizza you make for that first warm-weather get-together when everything starts to turn green and your favorite campground opens again. Don't forget to pack a portable grill with a lid, as you'll need one to properly melt the cheeses while the bottom crisps up.

GRILLED PIZZA PRIMAVERA

MAKES 4 SERVINGS

1 pound (450 g) Homemade Pizza Dough (page 146) or store-bought pizza dough

6 medium asparagus spears, trimmed (about ¼ pound/113 g)

½ small head broccoli florets (about ¼ pound/113 g)

4 scallions

Olive oil spray

½ cup (120 ml) No-Cook Pizza Sauce (page 147) or store-bought pizza sauce

1 cup (113 g) shredded mozzarella cheese

¼ cup (36 g) shelled English peas or thawed frozen peas

¼ cup (25 g) grated Parmesan cheese

Note: A pair of metal tongs works best for lifting and checking the crust for doneness, turning it over, and dragging the pizza off the grill.

Bring the chilled pizza dough to room temperature for about 30 minutes. Prepare a grill for high heat.

Lightly spray the asparagus, broccoli, and scallions with oil. Grill the vegetables until tender and charred all over, 3 to 5 minutes, turning frequently. Transfer the vegetables to a cutting board as they are cooked and chop into bite-size pieces. Keep the chopped vegetables near the grill for easy topping later.

Divide the dough in half and shape into 2 smooth balls. Working with the first ball of dough, flatten and stretch it into an 8-inch (20-cm) round. Lightly mist it with oil and place the dough, oiled side down, over direct heat. Cover and grill until the bottom is lightly browned with good grill marks and the crust is barely cooked on top, about 2 minutes. Mist the crust with oil and turn it over.

Working quickly, spread half the sauce over it, followed by half each of the mozzarella, grilled vegetables, and peas. Top with half the Parmesan, then cover and continue grilling until the crust is crisp and browned and the cheeses are melted, 3 to 5 minutes more.

Periodically check the pizza to ensure the crust isn't scorching, and reduce the heat if necessary. Repeat the process for making the second pizza.

Family-style meals have always been a favorite of mine, especially in camp when the vibe is casual and the chatter is plentiful. When whole red snapper is served this way, friends and family are encouraged to pick at the fish and pass around plates, making for a more dynamic and intimate feast. At the end of the meal, I like to carve out the cheeks and offer them to my guests of honor. A delicious delicacy often discarded, fish cheeks are smooth and buttery, almost like scallops.

GRILLED RED SNAPPER WITH CHERMOULA AND COUSCOUS

MAKES 4 SERVINGS

1 (3-pound/1,360 g) whole red snapper, cleaned and scaled

1½ cups (350 ml) Chermoula (page 164), divided

Kosher salt and ground black pepper

3 medium lemons, divided

1 cup (240 ml) chicken broth

1 cup (175 g) uncooked instant couscous

Let the snapper come to room temperature for about 30 minutes.

Meanwhile, prepare a grill for medium-high heat. Reserve 1 cup (240 ml) of the chermoula for serving.

Pat the snapper dry with paper towels, then cut a few deep slits in each side, slicing almost through to the bone. Rub the snapper inside and out with the remaining ½ cup (110 ml) chermoula, working it well into the slits. Lightly season with salt and pepper. Slice 1 of the lemons into rounds and stuff it into the cavity.

Place the snapper on the grill and cook for about 20 minutes, turning once, until the fish flakes easily and the meat closest to the bone is opaque but still moist. The snapper will continue to cook for 1 to 2 minutes off the heat, so start checking at the 15- to 18-minute mark and remove it from the grill when it's just shy of being done.

In the meantime, bring the broth to a boil in a small saucepan. Remove the saucepan from the heat and stir in the couscous. Cover and let sit for about 10 minutes, until all of the liquid is absorbed. Fluff the couscous with a fork.

Transfer the snapper to a cutting board or serving dish and serve with the couscous, reserved chermoula, and remaining 2 lemons, cut into wedges.

3 SIMPLE STEPS TO A STICK-FREE SURFACE ON A GRILL

1. **Heat It:** A blazing hot grate helps food remnants release more easily.
2. **Clean It:** Scrape the hot grate thoroughly and let the burnt bits fall into the flames.
3. **Oil It:** Season the hot grate with a light coating of oil.

Food still sticking? Don't try to flip too soon—meats and vegetables will release naturally after they get a good sear on one side. For more tips on mastering the grill, see page 25.

For me, some of the best things about summer are weekends spent camping along the coast: the long, lazy days, the thrill of diving into a shockingly cold wave and feeling like a kid again, the roaring beach bonfires, and the simple, satisfying meals cooked over them. When fresh, seasonal ingredients are picked at the peak of ripeness, little more is needed for maximum flavor in these summer vegetable and salmon packets.

SUMMER VEGETABLE AND SALMON PACKETS

MAKES 4 SERVINGS

Olive oil spray

4 (6-ounce/170 g) salmon fillets

2 cups (300 g) cherry tomatoes, halved

2 medium shallots, sliced

1 medium zucchini, sliced

1 medium bell pepper, cored and diced

4 cloves garlic, minced

Balsamic vinegar

Kosher salt and ground black pepper

Handful of basil leaves, thinly sliced

Prepare a grill over high heat.

Mist 4 sheets of aluminum foil with oil. Place a salmon fillet in the center of each sheet, then top each fillet with one-fourth of the tomatoes, shallots, zucchini, bell pepper, and garlic. Add a drizzle of vinegar and sprinkle with a hefty pinch of salt and pepper.

Bring the sides of the foil up, then fold the top over tightly to seal, leaving enough room for heat and steam to circulate inside the packets. Grill the packets for about 15 minutes, until the fish is flaky and the vegetables are tender. Garnish with basil before serving.

Bright and tangy, lemon and dill perk up the flavor of a simple, stress-free, mess-free foil pack. If you've been too intimidated to make fish for fear of sticking, overcooking, or undercooking, foil packs will become your go-to grilling technique in camp and even at home. It's one of my favorite ways to cook fish, since it stays moist in its own juices and there's no worry about scraping half the flesh off the grill. I like to use halibut but you can try any firm-fleshed fish in this recipe, such as cod, sea bass, or snapper.

FOIL-BAKED FISH WITH LEMON-DILL COUSCOUS

MAKES 4 SERVINGS

2 large lemons, divided

1½ cups (360 ml) chicken broth, divided

1 cup (175 g) uncooked pearl couscous

1 teaspoon dried dill

Olive oil spray

16 medium asparagus spears, trimmed and cut in half (about 1 pound/450 g)

4 (6-ounce/170 g) halibut fillets

¼ cup (56 g) butter, cut into small pieces

Kosher salt and ground black pepper

Note: Pearl couscous is also known as Israeli couscous.

Prepare a grill over high heat.

Slice 1 of the lemons into 8 rounds. In a medium bowl, combine 1 cup (240 ml) of the broth with the couscous, the juice from the remaining 1 lemon, and the dill.

Mist 4 sheets of aluminum foil with oil and bring all the sides up to form a bowl. Mound one-fourth of the couscous, including the liquid, in the center of each bowl. Top each mound with 8 asparagus halves, 1 halibut fillet, a few pieces of butter, a hefty pinch of salt and pepper, and 2 lemon slices.

Pour one-fourth of the remaining ½ cup (120 ml) broth into each bowl. Fold the foil tightly together on top to seal, leaving room inside each packet for heat and steam to circulate. Grill the packets for about 15 minutes, until the halibut is cooked through and the couscous and asparagus are tender.

As a coastal dweller, I love a good seafood boil. My local fishmonger serves a steaming pile of Cajun-spiced seafood and starch on stacks of newspaper, complete with plastic bibs, crusty bread, and bottles of hot sauce alongside. These easy foil packs recreate that experience in camp, minus the big pot, the big mess, and the overeager pelicans hovering over your table! (Unless you're camping seaside, that is.) Serve the foil packs with slices of grilled bread to soak up all the buttery juices.

TIN FOIL SEAFOOD BOIL

MAKES 4 SERVINGS

Olive oil spray

1 large lemon, sliced into 8 rounds

16 large shrimp, peeled and deveined (16/20 count, about ¾ pound/340 g)

8 sea scallops (about ½ pound/226 g)

2 ears corn, cut into quarters

8 new potatoes, halved or quartered (about ¾ pound/340 g)

3 links andouille sausage, cut into ¼-inch slices (about 9 ounces/255 g)

1 cup (240 ml) beer, dry white wine, or chicken broth

¼ cup (56 g) butter, cut into small pieces

1 tablespoon Old Bay Seasoning

Prepare a grill over high heat.

Lightly spray 4 sheets of aluminum foil with oil. Mound one-fourth of the lemon, shrimp, scallops, corn, potatoes, and sausage in the middle of each sheet, then bring all four sides of the foil up to form a bowl.

Pour an equal amount of beer into each packet, followed by a few pats of butter and a sprinkle of Old Bay Seasoning. Fold the foil tightly together on top to seal, leaving room inside the packet for steam and heat to circulate. Grill the packets for about 15 minutes, until the seafood is cooked through and the vegetables are tender.

✧ MIX IT UP ✧

Clams and fish work equally well in these foil packs, so feel free to add as much variety of seafood as you want; they'll cook in the same amount of time as the shrimp and scallops.

There's a lot of garlic in this recipe, and rightly so for a recipe inspired by gambas al ajillo (garlic shrimp), one of my favorite Spanish tapas. It's bold in flavor but simple in preparation, making it a go-to for a great camp feast (especially because you'll have wine left over for the meal). The orzo is optional, but I like having a starch to soak up the silky tomato sauce—you can try couscous instead, or serve it tapas-style with a loaf of crusty bread for a larger group.

GARLICKY SHRIMP WITH OLIVE OIL, TOMATOES, AND ORZO

MAKES 4 SERVINGS

FOR THE ORZO
2 cups (473 ml) chicken broth

1 cup (210 g) uncooked orzo

1 tablespoon butter

FOR THE SHRIMP
¼ cup (120 ml) olive oil

8 cloves garlic, thinly sliced

3 cups halved cherry tomatoes

½ teaspoon kosher salt

½ teaspoon red pepper flakes

1 cup (240 ml) dry white wine

1¼ pounds (566 g) large shrimp, peeled and deveined (16/20 count)

Handful of fresh parsley leaves, chopped

To make the orzo, bring the broth to a boil in a small saucepan. Add the orzo and simmer until all of the liquid is absorbed and the orzo is tender and chewy, about 10 minutes, stirring occasionally. (If the orzo is still crunchy after absorbing all the broth, add a little water and continue cooking for a few more minutes until it is al dente.) Remove the saucepan from the heat, stir in the butter until melted, and keep warm.

Meanwhile, to make the shrimp, heat the oil in a large skillet over medium-high heat. Add the garlic and cook until fragrant, 1 to 2 minutes. Add the tomatoes, salt, and red pepper flakes and cook until the tomatoes start to burst and soften, 3 to 4 minutes, stirring occasionally. Pour in the wine and bring to a boil. Reduce the heat and simmer until the liquid is reduced by almost half. Add the shrimp and cook until they are opaque, 2 to 3 minutes.

Serve the shrimp and tomatoes on a bed of orzo and scatter parsley on top.

✧ USE IT UP ✧

Leftover parsley can be used to garnish Grilled Corn on the Cob, 4 Ways (page 120), One-Pot Penne alla Vodka (page 178), or Dutch Oven Old-School Lasagna (page 179).

Skirt steak is an ideal cut of beef for the sizzle of a grill. It's long and thin, intensely flavorful, and takes to high heat very well, making it a quick and satisfying meal to fix in camp. Here, its richness and toughness are balanced by the sweetness and tenderness of baby bok choy (sometimes called dwarf bok choy or dwarf pak choi). The steak is done in the same amount of time as the vegetables, so if your grill is able to accommodate all that food at once, you can have a plate of dinner in your lap in less than 15 minutes.

GRILLED SKIRT STEAK AND BABY BOK CHOY WITH GINGER-SOY BUTTER

MAKES 4 SERVINGS

1 (1½-pound/680 g) skirt steak, cut in half (see Note)

Kosher salt and ground black pepper

8 small heads baby bok choy, halved lengthwise (about 1½ pounds/680 g)

Olive oil spray

Ginger-Soy Butter (page 161)

Note: If skirt steak isn't available, flank steak is a fine substitute. It tends to be a little thicker than skirt steak, so you might need to increase the total grilling time by 1 to 2 minutes.

Prepare a grill over medium-high heat.

Season the steak liberally with salt and pepper. Place the steak on the hottest part of the grill and cook for 2 to 3 minutes on each side, until nicely charred and medium-rare. Transfer the steak to a cutting board and let rest for 10 minutes.

Meanwhile, lightly spray the bok choy with oil and season with salt and pepper. Grill the bok choy for 8 to 10 minutes, turning occasionally, until the vegetables are crisp-tender with good grill marks.

Thinly slice the steak against the grain. Serve the steak and bok choy with a few pats of butter on top.

Compound Butters

For a camp cook, compound butters (butters that have been softened and com-
bined with aromatics, seasonings, and/or acid) make some of the most useful
and flavorful sauces for seared and grilled meats, fish, shellfish, and vegetables.
The combination of fat, smoke, herbs, and spices never fails to elevate a meal and
make it seem like you spent more time on it than you actually did. Compound but-
ters can simply be melted onto hot food for instant flavor or used as a base for
other sauces. Store a few in the freezer and you'll always have a great garnish or
condiment ready to go.

ALL RECIPES ON PAGE 161 MAKE ABOUT ½ CUP (113 G)

Basic Method

In a small bowl, stir together all of the ingredients until well combined.
Spoon the butter mixture onto a sheet of plastic wrap or waxed paper
and shape into a log about 1½ inches (4 cm) in diameter. Roll up the
log, twist the ends to secure, and chill for up to 1 week. (Alternatively,
you can freeze the compound butter for up to 6 months and slice off
sections as needed.)

Note: I use salted butter for all of these recipes, so if you have unsalted butter,
adjust for taste and add salt as needed.

Garlic-Herb Butter

This fresh and versatile butter amps up omelets, pasta, potatoes, and all types of meats, poultry, fish, and shellfish. Keep a log in your freezer at all times for last-minute needs.

½ cup (113 g) butter, softened

½ cup (25 g) minced fresh herbs (such as basil, cilantro, parsley, thyme, oregano, and/or chives)

4 cloves garlic, minced

½ teaspoon ground black pepper

Tarragon Butter

The distinct flavor of tarragon works well with seafood, particularly baked fish and seared scallops, and spring vegetables like asparagus, green peas, carrots, and cauliflower.

½ cup (113 g) butter, softened

2 tablespoons minced fresh tarragon

1 teaspoon minced chives

Juice of ½ medium lemon

Sun-Dried Tomato and Basil Butter

With its tangy, savory, and earthy flavors, this butter melds beautifully with pasta, corn on the cob, grilled bread, and grilled vegetable skewers.

½ cup (113 g) butter, softened

¼ cup (43 g) finely chopped oil-packed sun-dried tomatoes

2 tablespoons minced fresh basil

2 cloves garlic, minced

Ginger-Soy Butter

Put this umami butter on skirt steak (page 159) and other grilled meats and poultry, or try it on mushrooms, root vegetables, Asian vegetables, and Asian-inspired soups or noodle bowls.

½ cup (113 g) butter, softened

¼ cup (60 ml) soy sauce

1 tablespoon grated ginger

2 cloves garlic, minced

Juice of ½ medium lemon

Gorgonzola Butter

This rich and creamy butter pairs perfectly with baked potatoes, as well as skirt steak, flank steak, lamb chops, and other intensely flavored meats.

½ cup (113 g) butter, softened

½ cup (56 g) crumbled Gorgonzola cheese

2 scallions, finely chopped

Honey Butter

Compound butters don't have to be savory—sweet ones like this turn ordinary toast, biscuits, and croissants into things you look forward to in the morning.

½ cup (113 g) butter, softened

2 tablespoons honey

¼ teaspoon ground cinnamon

You can eat a salad tomorrow. Tonight, it's all about meat and potatoes. Wrap a few spuds in foil, toss a steak on the grill, and crack open some cold ones while you kick back in your camp chair. It's the kind of dinner you don't have to fuss over, since the fingerlings do their own thing and the steak is done in a flash. Finish them off the grill with a generous drizzle of herby, garlicky, tangy chimichurri for a little zing. If you have leftover chimichurri, spoon it over eggs in the morning; if you have leftover potatoes as well, turn them into a chimichurri breakfast hash.

GRILLED FLANK STEAK AND FINGERLING POTATOES WITH CHIMICHURRI

MAKES 4 SERVINGS

Olive oil spray

20 fingerling potatoes (about 1½ pounds/680 g)

4 medium shallots, sliced

Kosher salt and ground black pepper

1 (1½-pound/680-g) flank steak, cut in half

Chimichurri (page 164)

Prepare a grill over high heat.

Mist 4 sheets of aluminum foil with oil. Mound an equal portion of potatoes and shallots in the center of each sheet, spray with a little more oil, and sprinkle with a hefty pinch of salt and pepper. Fold the sides of the foil up to form a pouch and seal the top, leaving room for steam and heat to circulate inside. Grill the packets for about 20 minutes, until the potatoes are tender.

Meanwhile, season the steak liberally with salt and pepper. Place the steak on the hottest part of the grill and cook for 2 to 3 minutes on each side, until well charred and medium-rare. Transfer the steak to a cutting board and let rest for 10 minutes.

Thinly slice the steak against the grain. Spoon the chimichurri over the steak and potatoes before serving.

CHIMICHURRI AND CHERMOULA

When I'm stuck on how to make a meal more special, or simply want to add some zing to my food, I usually reach for one of these sauces. Though they come from wildly different parts of the world—chimichurri (right) is a traditional drizzle of Argentina, while chermoula (left) is a staple in North Africa—they've crossed over into countless recipes for their versatility, punchy flavors, and ease of preparation. Bring a jar to camp and you'll never have trouble deciding what to do about dinner.

Chimichurri

Sharp, tangy, and garlicky, chimichurri seems made for the smoky, savory meats of a campfire grill. A drizzle over seared steak and potatoes (page 162) is my favorite way to use it, but you can also try it on fish, vegetables, eggs, or salads.

MAKES 2 CUPS (475 ML)

2 cups (100 g) packed fresh parsley, minced

3 tablespoons minced garlic

3 tablespoons minced fresh oregano

1½ tablespoons red pepper flakes

1 to 1¼ cups (240 to 300 ml) olive oil

¼ cup (60 ml) red wine vinegar

Stir together all of the ingredients in a small bowl until well combined. Use less oil for a chunkier texture, or more oil for a looser consistency. Transfer the chimichurri to a lidded container. Let stand overnight at room temperature for the flavors to marry, then chill for up to 3 weeks. Bring the chimichurri to room temperature before serving.

Note: Don't worry if the parsley starts to oxidize (brown) over time. As any Argentinean will tell you, a sign of a good, well-aged chimichurri is when it's turned a dull army green with a slightly murky appearance.

Chermoula

Warm, smoky, and savory with a touch of brightness, chermoula is traditionally served with grilled fish (page 150) but works well on other types of seafood, meat, and vegetables, particularly if they have a healthy bit of char on them.

MAKES 1½ CUPS (350 ML)

2 cups (100 g) packed fresh parsley

2 cups (100 g) packed fresh cilantro

4 cloves garlic

1 tablespoon ground cumin

1 tablespoon ground coriander

1 teaspoon hot paprika

1 teaspoon kosher salt

Juice of 1 medium lemon

½ cup (120 ml) olive oil

Add the parsley, cilantro, garlic, cumin, coriander, paprika, salt, and lemon juice to the bowl of a food processor and pulse until finely chopped and well combined, scraping down the sides of the bowl as necessary. With the motor running, pour the oil through the feeding tube and process until a smooth sauce forms. Transfer the chermoula to a lidded container and chill for up to 3 days.

2 pounds (900 g) skinless boneless chicken thighs, cut into 1-by-2-inch (2-by-5-cm) strips (see Note)

2 tablespoons Moroccan Spice Blend (page 71)

3 cups (540 g) chopped tomatoes

½ cup finely chopped red onion

Handful of fresh mint leaves, finely chopped

Kosher salt and ground black pepper

Juice of ½ medium lemon

Olive oil

Chermoula (page 164)

Note: To keep the chicken pieces from rotating on the skewer, cut each thigh into 1-by-2-inch (2-by-5-cm) strips. Fold each strip in half and pierce the skewer through both ends.

✧ USE IT UP ✧

Fresh mint is too good to let go to waste—use it up in Thai Quinoa Salad with a Trio of Fresh Herbs (page 75) as well as in place of (or in addition to) the fresh basil in Stone Fruit Salsa (page 108) or Summer Ale Sangria with Ginger and Peach (page 194).

Skewers can sometimes feel uninspired. Chalk it up to one too many zucchini coins and onion wedges in my day, and chunks of chicken breasts charred out of all their moisture. But these skewers, full of succulent dark-meat chicken coated in warm savory spices, are tender, full of flavor, and so simple to make. Here, they're balanced with fresh herbal chermoula and a bright tangy salad that celebrates summer tomatoes. Try to find the ripest, sweetest varieties, as their juices will marry beautifully with the olive oil.

MOROCCAN-SPICED CHICKEN SKEWERS WITH CHERMOULA AND TOMATO-MINT SALAD

MAKES 4 SERVINGS

At Home
Place the chicken in a large bowl, sprinkle with the spice blend, and toss to coat thoroughly. Transfer the chicken to a resealable plastic bag, squeeze out the excess air, and chill for at least 2 hours and up to 24 hours.

In Camp
Prepare a grill over medium-high heat.

Meanwhile, combine the tomatoes, onion, mint, and a hefty pinch of salt and pepper in a serving bowl. Drizzle with the lemon juice and oil to taste and toss to coat. Set aside until ready to serve.

Thread the chicken onto skewers and grill until cooked through and nicely charred all over, 8 to 12 minutes, turning occasionally.

Serve the chicken with a drizzle of chermoula and the tomato-mint salad on the side.

5 skin-on, bone-in chicken thighs (about 2 pounds/900 g)

Kosher salt and ground black pepper

2 teaspoons ground cumin, divided

2 tablespoons olive oil

1 medium yellow onion, chopped

1 medium bell pepper, cored and chopped

1 poblano pepper, chopped

4 cloves garlic, minced

1 teaspoon dried oregano

1 teaspoon ground turmeric

1 bay leaf

1 (8-ounce/226 g) can tomato sauce

1½ cups (300 g) uncooked long-grain white rice

1½ cups (350 ml) chicken broth

1 cup (240 ml) beer

1 cup (145 g) thawed frozen peas

Handful of fresh cilantro leaves, chopped

✧ USE IT UP ✧

Put those leftover peas on Grilled Pizza Primavera (page 149). The rest of the cilantro can be used in Grilled Guacamole (page 106), Mexican Shrimp Cocktail (page 123), Mexican Street Corn Salad (page 122), Thai Quinoa Salad with a Trio of Fresh Herbs (page 75), Market-Fresh Taco Salad with Creamy Cilantro-Lime Dressing (page 80), Grilled Shrimp Tacos with Corn and Tomato Salsa (page 98), Foil-Pack Salmon with Pineapple Salsa (page 101), or Red Lentil Soup with Carrot and Cumin (page 138).

You might notice that the Spanish name for this classic comfort dish, arroz con pollo, means "rice with chicken," and not the other way around. That's because arroz con pollo is all about the deeply flavorful yellow rice made with sofrito, an aromatic mixture of pepper, onion, tomato, and spices cooked down into a thick sauce. While sofrito is fairly standard across most recipes, every variation of arroz con pollo gets its personality from the region in which it originates—in this case, the Caribbean.

CUBAN RICE WITH CHICKEN

MAKES 5 SERVINGS

Season the chicken liberally with salt and pepper, and sprinkle 1 teaspoon of the cumin all over.

Heat a stockpot over medium-high heat and swirl in the oil. Add the chicken in a single layer and cook undisturbed until browned on both sides, 10 to 12 minutes, turning once. Transfer the chicken to a plate.

Let the stockpot and chicken juices reheat and add the onion, bell pepper, poblano pepper, garlic, oregano, turmeric, bay leaf, tomato sauce, and remaining 1 teaspoon cumin. Cook until the vegetables are crisp-tender, about 3 minutes, stirring occasionally. Add the rice, broth, and beer and stir to coat the rice thoroughly. Bring the mixture to a boil, stirring frequently to submerge the rice in liquid.

Return the chicken to the stockpot and nestle the thighs, skin side up, on the rice and vegetables. Reduce the heat, cover, and simmer until most of the liquid is absorbed, the rice is tender, and the chicken is cooked through, about 20 minutes. Stir in the peas and continue cooking, uncovered, until the peas are heated through and all of the liquid is absorbed, about 5 minutes more. Remove from the heat and let stand 10 minutes before serving.

Discard the bay leaf. Garnish with cilantro and serve each chicken thigh on a bed of rice.

FOR THE PICKLES

⅔ cup (160 ml) white vinegar

⅔ cup (160 ml) water

⅓ cup (67 g) sugar

2 tablespoons sriracha

1 medium English cucumber, thinly sliced on the diagonal (about ½ pound/226 g)

FOR THE STEAK

½ cup (120 ml) soy sauce

¼ cup (60 ml) rice vinegar

2 tablespoons minced ginger

2 tablespoons sriracha

2 tablespoons toasted sesame oil

2 tablespoons sugar

2 scallions, finely chopped

4 cloves garlic, minced

1 (1½-pound/680 g) flank steak, cut in half

FOR SERVING

2¼ (535 ml) cups water

1½ cups (300 g) uncooked long-grain white rice

Lettuce leaves

Note: Depending on the variety of rice, cooking time may be more or less than stated in the recipe. When in doubt, follow the instructions on the package as to how much liquid to use and how long to cook.

The smell of a good steak searing in the open air is one of my favorite things about cooking in camp. Coupled with a robust sauce, like this Korean bulgogi-style marinade, it's guaranteed to be a hit with your hungry campmates. And it's fun to eat too. Each person makes his or her own lettuce-leaf bundles with rice, steak, and pickles, so serve it all up family-style.

KOREAN FLANK STEAK WITH SRIRACHA-PICKLED CUCUMBERS

MAKES 4 SERVINGS

At Home

To make the pickles, stir together the vinegar, water, sugar, and sriracha in a small bowl until the sugar is dissolved. Pack the cucumbers into a lidded container and pour in the brine. Chill overnight and up to 2 weeks.

To make the steak, whisk together the soy sauce, vinegar, ginger, sriracha, sesame oil, sugar, scallions, and garlic in a small bowl until well blended. Reserve half the sauce in a lidded container and chill. Add the remaining sauce and the steak to a resealable plastic bag and shake to coat thoroughly. Squeeze out the excess air, then chill overnight and up to 24 hours.

In Camp

To serve, bring the water to a boil in a small saucepan. Stir in the rice. Reduce the heat, cover, and simmer until all of the liquid is absorbed and the rice is tender and fluffy, 15 to 20 minutes.

Meanwhile, prepare a grill over medium-high heat.

Place the steak on the hottest part of the grill and cook for 2 to 4 minutes on each side for medium-rare. Transfer to a cutting board and let rest for 10 minutes. Thinly slice the steak against the grain.

Drizzle the steak with the reserved sauce brought from home. Serve with the lettuce leaves, rice, and pickles.

The chicken is moist and savory. The rice is fluffy and subtly sweet. But the star of this recipe is the Thai peanut sauce, which gives all the ingredients that added oomph. It's rich and smooth with just a touch of heat, and aside from chicken, it pairs well with a multitude of other meats and vegetables. Make the sauce at home ahead of your camping trip and vary this dish by trying it with baked salmon, stir-fried pork, or grilled vegetables.

CHICKEN IN THAI PEANUT SAUCE WITH COCONUT RICE

MAKES 4 SERVINGS

1 (14-ounce/415-ml) can coconut milk

1 cup (240 ml) water

1½ cups (300 g) uncooked long-grain white rice

Handful of cilantro leaves, chopped, plus more for garnishing

2 tablespoons olive oil

8 skinless boneless chicken thighs, cut into bite-size pieces (about 1½ pounds/680 g)

Kosher salt and ground black pepper

1½ cups (350 ml) Thai Peanut Sauce (opposite page)

Chopped dry-roasted peanuts

In a small saucepan over medium-high heat, bring the coconut milk and water to a boil. Stir in the rice and cilantro. Reduce the heat, cover, and simmer until all of the liquid is absorbed and the rice is tender, about 15 minutes. Let stand, covered, for 10 minutes before serving.

Note: Depending on the variety of rice, cooking time may be more or less than stated in the recipe. When in doubt, follow the instructions on the package as to how much liquid to use and how long to cook.

Meanwhile, heat a large skillet over medium-high heat and add the oil. Sprinkle the chicken with salt and pepper and arrange the pieces in a single layer in the skillet. Cook undisturbed until the bottoms are browned, 3 to 4 minutes. Toss the chicken around and continue cooking until the meat is cooked through, 6 to 8 minutes more, stirring occasionally.

Pour in the peanut sauce and stir to coat the chicken. Cook until the sauce is heated through, 2 to 3 minutes.

Fluff the rice with a fork. Divide the rice and chicken among 4 plates and garnish with chopped cilantro and peanuts.

Thai Peanut Sauce

Homemade authentic Thai peanut sauce can be intimidating with its long list of exotic herbs and spices, but luckily, most of them are found in commercial Thai red curry paste (available in the ethnic food aisle of well-stocked supermarkets). Use this shortcut recipe for Thai satay dishes as well as curries, soups, and noodles; as a savory drizzle for grilled fish and meats; or as a dipping sauce for summer rolls and Lettuce Cups with Sesame-Soy Chicken (page 84).

MAKES 2 ½ CUPS (585 ML)

1 (14-ounce/415-ml) can coconut milk

½ cup (135 g) creamy natural peanut butter

3 tablespoons Thai red curry paste

2 tablespoons cider vinegar

1 tablespoon sugar

1 teaspoon kosher salt

Whisk together all of the ingredients in a small saucepan over medium-high heat. Simmer for 3 to 5 minutes, until the sauce is smooth and well blended. Remove the saucepan from the heat and let cool to room temperature. Transfer to a lidded container and chill for up to 2 weeks.

Orzotto is a specialty of northeastern Italy that uses barley in place of rice for risotto, but here we use orzo, a small rice-shaped pasta, for less stirring and speedier cooking. In fact, orzo means "barley" in Italian, as the pasta resembles a large grain. It's prepared in much the same way as risotto rice: by lightly toasting in the pan, then simmering in wine and broth. As the orzo cooks, it releases its starch and gives the dish a thick and velvety texture reminiscent of classic risotto.

ORZOTTO WITH CHICKEN, MUSHROOM, AND LEEK

MAKES 4 SERVINGS

2 tablespoons olive oil, divided

8 skinless boneless chicken thighs (about 1½ pounds/680 g)

Kosher salt and ground black pepper

6 medium cremini mushrooms, sliced

1 small leek, halved lengthwise and thinly sliced (about ¼ pound/113 g)

1 cup (225 g) uncooked orzo

¼ cup (60 ml) dry red wine

2 cups (475 ml) chicken broth

½ teaspoon Italian seasoning

⅓ cup (33 g) grated Parmesan cheese

In a 12-inch (30-cm) skillet over medium-high heat, drizzle 1 tablespoon of the oil. Season the chicken with salt and pepper, and cook for about 5 minutes, until browned on one side. Flip the chicken and continue cooking until the meat is no longer pink in the center, about 10 minutes. Transfer the chicken to a plate and keep warm.

In the same skillet, swirl in the remaining 1 tablespoon oil and add the mushrooms in a single layer. Cook undisturbed until browned on the bottom, 1 to 2 minutes. Add the leek and a hefty pinch of salt and pepper and cook until the leek is tender, 2 to 3 minutes, stirring occasionally.

Stir in the orzo and cook for about 2 minutes until lightly toasted. Add the wine and cook until the liquid is almost evaporated. Add the broth and Italian seasoning and bring to a boil.

Reduce the heat, cover, and simmer for 10 to 12 minutes, stirring occasionally, until all of the liquid is absorbed and the orzo is tender. Stir in the Parmesan. Place the chicken on top of the orzo, cover, and heat through for 2 to 3 minutes. Divide the orzo and chicken among 4 plates and serve.

Chicken fajitas have always been a crowd-pleaser on my camping trips for their ease of cooking. But it's good to mix things up a bit, especially if you can keep the dirty dishes to a minimum. This version has all the makings of fajitas—the chicken, peppers, tomatoes, and onion, all seasoned with a Mexican-style spice blend—but incorporates them into a hearty pasta dish that cooks in the same skillet, no draining required. (A skillet with high sides is recommended.)

ONE-PAN CHICKEN FAJITA PASTA

MAKES 4 SERVINGS

1 pound (450 g) skinless boneless chicken breasts, cut into bite-size pieces

2 tablespoons South-of-the-Border Seasoning (page 175), divided

2 tablespoons olive oil, divided

1 medium yellow onion, diced

4 cloves garlic, minced

2 medium bell peppers, cored and diced

1 poblano pepper, diced

3 cups (340 g) uncooked rotini pasta

2 cups (475 ml) chicken broth

1 (15-ounce/425 g) can diced tomatoes

⅓ cup (75 g) sour cream

Handful of cilantro leaves, chopped

1 large lime, cut into wedges

In a bowl, coat the chicken with 1 tablespoon of the seasoning.

In a large skillet over medium-high heat, swirl 1 tablespoon of the oil around and add the chicken in a single layer. Cook undisturbed until browned on the bottom, 2 to 3 minutes. Stir the chicken around and continue cooking until the meat is no longer pink in the center, 2 to 3 minutes more. Transfer the chicken to a plate.

Let the skillet reheat and add the remaining 1 tablespoon oil. Add the onion and garlic and cook until the onion starts to turn translucent, 2 to 3 minutes. Add the bell peppers, poblano pepper, and remaining 1 tablespoon seasoning and cook until the vegetables are tender, 3 to 5 minutes, stirring occasionally. Transfer the vegetables to the plate of chicken.

Add the pasta, broth, and tomatoes to the skillet and bring to a boil. Reduce the heat and simmer until most of the liquid is absorbed and the pasta is al dente, 10 to 12 minutes, stirring frequently. Return the chicken and vegetables to the skillet and heat through for about 3 minutes. Stir in the sour cream and cilantro until well combined.

Serve with lime wedges.

South-of-the-Border Seasoning

You know those little packets of taco or fajita seasoning that you buy at the store? This replaces them! It's a spicy and smoky mix that adds serious zip to ground beef or skirt steak. You can also use it as a dry rub or sprinkle it on grilled chicken, shrimp, and vegetable skewers when you want some south-of-the-border flair.

MAKES ¼ CUP (25 G)

4 teaspoons chile powder

2 teaspoons kosher salt

2 teaspoons smoked paprika

1 teaspoon sugar

1 teaspoon ground cumin

1 teaspoon garlic powder

1 teaspoon onion powder

½ teaspoon cayenne pepper

Combine all of the ingredients in a small bowl. Transfer to a resealable plastic bag or lidded container and store in a dry, cool place for up to 6 months.

I'm a fan of one-pot pasta recipes at home, and in camp, they're even better because the convenience of washing only one pot in the evening, under the glow of my headlamp, cannot be beat. This traditional dish looks deceptively simple but offers a mélange of flavors in one bite. It also lends itself to lots of easy variations, whether you want another pinch of red pepper flakes for a feistier sauce or a handful of peas, prosciutto, or shrimp tossed in near the end of cooking.

ONE-POT PENNE ALLA VODKA

MAKES 4 SERVINGS

2 tablespoons olive oil

2 medium shallots, chopped

4 cloves garlic, minced

1 tablespoon tomato paste

⅓ cup (80 ml) vodka

1 (28-ounce/800 g) can diced tomatoes

½ teaspoon kosher salt

¼ teaspoon red pepper flakes

5 cups (450 g) uncooked penne pasta

2 cups (475 ml) chicken broth

½ cup (120 ml) heavy cream

Handful of fresh parsley leaves, chopped

Grated Parmesan cheese

Heat a stockpot over medium-high heat and add the oil, shallots, and garlic. Cook until the shallots start to turn translucent, 2 to 3 minutes. Add the tomato paste and cook for about 1 minute, until the shallots are thoroughly coated. Pour in the vodka and cook until the liquid is reduced by almost half. Add the tomatoes, salt, and red pepper flakes and simmer until the sauce starts to thicken, about 10 minutes, stirring occasionally. Add the pasta and broth and bring to a boil.

Reduce the heat and simmer until most of the liquid is absorbed and the pasta is al dente, 12 to 15 minutes, stirring frequently. Remove the stockpot from the heat and stir in the heavy cream.

Serve with a sprinkle of parsley and Parmesan on top.

✧ USE IT UP ✧

No need to carry that half-empty can of tomato paste back home with you. Use it up in Red Lentil Soup with Carrot and Cumin (page 138), Five-Alarm Three-Bean Chili (page 142), or Dutch Oven Old-School Lasagna (page 179). Leftover parsley can go on Grilled Corn on the Cob, 4 Ways (page 120), Garlicky Shrimp with Olive Oil, Tomatoes, and Orzo (page 158), or Dutch Oven Old-School Lasagna (page 179).

If your love for pizza leans toward deep and hearty crusts that can hold a lot of sauce and cheese, this dutch oven deep-dish pie is a camping delight. Though it has few ingredients, it pushes and pulls your taste buds in two directions at once with a bold contrast of flavors: spicy soppressata and sweet fennel, mild mozzarella and hot serrano. You can layer the toppings Chicago-style (that is, upside down, or finishing with sauce on top—even adding more sauce and cheese if that's your thing), but I love how it looks when the pizza is piping hot out of the oven with slices of fennel nestled in cheese. If you want less heat, try sweet soppressata; for more heat, add a sprinkle of red pepper flakes. (Pictured on page 178.)

DUTCH OVEN DEEP-DISH SOPPRESSATA AND FENNEL PIZZA

MAKES 3 SERVINGS

Olive oil spray

1 pound (450 g) Homemade Pizza Dough (page 146) or store-bought pizza dough

¾ cup (180 ml) No-Cook Pizza Sauce (page 148), or store-bought pizza sauce

2 cups (226 g) shredded mozzarella cheese

10 thin slices hot soppressata (about 2 ounces/56 g)

½ medium fennel bulb, thinly sliced

1 serrano pepper, thinly sliced

½ cup (113 g) ricotta cheese

Ground black pepper

Bring the chilled pizza dough to room temperature for about 30 minutes. Meanwhile, prepare a mound of wood coals, hardwood lump charcoal, or charcoal briquettes (see page 25).

Lightly spray a dutch oven with oil. Stretch and shape the dough into a 12-inch (30-cm) round. Press the dough into the oven, pushing 1 to 1½ inches (2 to 4 cm) up the sides to form a shallow bowl for the toppings. Spread the pizza sauce evenly over the dough, followed by the mozzarella, soppressata, fennel, and serrano. Dab small spoonfuls of ricotta on top, and sprinkle with a hefty pinch of pepper.

Move about a quart's worth of coals to the cooking pit and arrange them in a ring (see pages 32 to 34). Cover the oven, set it on the ring of coals, and place 2 rings of coals on the lid.

Bake over high heat for 30 to 40 minutes, until the crust is crisp and golden brown, the fennel is tender, and the mozzarella is melted. Replenish the coals as needed to maintain high heat and rotate the oven and lid halfway through for even cooking. Let stand, covered, for 10 minutes before slicing and serving.

RECIPE CONTINUES

THE DUTCH OVEN:
AN AMERICAN SYMBOL OF FAMILY

The timeless cast-iron cooking pot we know and love today has changed only slightly since its use in the early days by American pioneers. So important is the dutch oven to our culinary history—and the families that continue to use it, whether at home or in camp—that it was officially adopted as the State Cooking Implement in Texas in 2005, the State Historic Cooking Vessel in Arkansas in 2001, and the State Cooking Pot in Utah in 1997. In fact, the dutch oven is used by more families in Utah than in any other state! Perhaps it's because families have special significance in the state, and it's not uncommon for multiple generations to gather around a campfire with a meal made by the same dutch ovens passed down from their forbearers.

FOR THE MEAT SAUCE

½ pound (226 g) lean ground beef

1/2 pound (226 g) Italian sausage, casing removed

1 medium yellow onion, chopped

4 cloves garlic, minced

1 (28-ounce/800 g) can crushed tomatoes

1 (8-ounce/226 g) can tomato sauce

¼ cup (60 ml) dry red wine

1 tablespoon tomato paste

1 tablespoon Italian seasoning

1 teaspoon red pepper flakes

1 teaspoon kosher salt

½ teaspoon fennel seeds

¼ teaspoon ground black pepper

FOR THE CHEESE MIXTURE

2 large eggs

4½ cups (500 g) shredded mozzarella cheese, divided

2 cups (450 g) ricotta cheese

½ cup (50 g) grated Parmesan cheese, divided

½ cup (25 g) chopped fresh parsley leaves, plus more for garnishing

FOR THE LASAGNA

Olive oil spray

9 uncooked oven-ready lasagna noodles

3 cups packed baby spinach

Ooey gooey goodness was once only possible at home, in an oven, where layer upon layer of pasta, cheese, and sauce bubbled together in a tidy rectangular baking dish. But classic lasagna can now be had in camp! It might be round, but it's got all the flavors and layers you know and love. I use oven-ready noodles in this recipe to save the extra step of boiling them (and dirtying another pot . . . because who wants to do more dishes?).

DUTCH OVEN OLD-SCHOOL LASAGNA

MAKES 6 SERVINGS

To make the meat sauce, heat a large skillet over medium-high heat and add the ground beef and sausage. Flatten the meat, spread it across the skillet, and cook until browned on the bottom, about 5 minutes. Stir to break up the meat and continue cooking until browned all over, 3 to 5 minutes more. Add the onion and garlic and cook until the onion starts to turn translucent, 2 to 3 minutes. Stir in the tomatoes, tomato sauce, wine, tomato paste, Italian seasoning, red pepper flakes, salt, fennel seeds, and pepper. Bring the mixture to a boil, then reduce the heat and simmer until the sauce is thickened, about 15 minutes.

Meanwhile, prepare a mound of wood coals, hardwood lump charcoal, or charcoal briquettes (see page 25).

To make the cheese mixture, in a medium bowl, beat together the eggs, 4 cups (450 g) of the mozzarella, the ricotta, ¼ cup (25 g) of the Parmesan, and the parsley. Stir until well combined.

RECIPE CONTINUES

Note: Oven-ready lasagna noodles (sometimes called no-boil pasta) can be found in the dried pasta aisle of well-stocked supermarkets.

To assemble the lasagna, lightly spray a dutch oven with oil. Spoon one-third of the meat sauce into the oven, followed by one-third of the noodles, one-half of the cheese mixture, and one-half of the spinach. (Break the noodles into pieces to fit the oven.) Repeat with the remaining ingredients, finishing with a layer of meat sauce. Top with the remaining ½ cup (56 g) mozzarella and remaining ¼ cup (25 g) Parmesan.

Move about a quart's worth of coals to the cooking pit and arrange them in a ring (see pages 32 to 34). Cover the oven, set it on the ring of coals, and place 1½ rings of coals on the lid.

Bake over medium heat for about 30 minutes, until all of the cheeses are melted and the noodles are tender. Replenish the coals as needed to maintain medium heat and rotate the oven and lid halfway through for even cooking. Let stand, uncovered, for 10 minutes before serving. Garnish with parsley.

✧ USE IT UP ✧

What to do with the rest of that can of tomato paste? Use it up in Red Lentil Soup with Carrot and Cumin (page 138), One-Pot Penne alla Vodka (page 178), or Five-Alarm Three-Bean Chili (page 142). If you have parsley left over, put it on Grilled Corn on the Cob, 4 Ways (page 120), Garlicky Shrimp with Olive Oil, Tomatoes, and Orzo (page 158), or One-Pot Penne alla Vodka (page 178).

I make a version of this recipe at home that I call "oven-fried" chicken, as it has all the crispy bits I love about traditional fried chicken but without the deep-frying. In camp, a dutch oven serves the same purpose and it's a snap to clean up afterward—no grease splatters or excess oil to discard. You can adjust the seasonings in the chicken coating to suit your taste (perhaps a few pinches of cayenne pepper for added heat?) or swap out the kale and apple slaw for Grilled Coleslaw with Creamy Gorgonzola Vinaigrette (page 128).

DUTCH OVEN–BAKED BUTTERMILK CHICKEN WITH KALE AND APPLE SLAW

MAKES 4 SERVINGS

FOR THE CHICKEN

2 cups (475 ml) buttermilk

8 skin-on bone-in chicken thighs (about 3 pounds/1,360 g)

1 cup (240 g) all-purpose flour

1 cup (112 g) bread crumbs

1 tablespoon garlic powder

1 tablespoon onion powder

Olive oil spray

1 tablespoon butter

Smoked paprika

At Home

To make the chicken, place the buttermilk and chicken in a resealable plastic bag, shake to coat thoroughly, then squeeze out the excess air and seal the bag. Chill for at least 2 hours and up to 24 hours.

In a separate resealable plastic bag, combine the flour, bread crumbs, garlic powder, and onion powder. Store in a dry, cool place until ready to use.

In Camp

One by one, drain the excess brine off the chicken and transfer the chicken to the bag of flour mixture. Coat the chicken thoroughly and let rest in a wide, shallow dish for about 30 minutes.

Meanwhile, prepare a mound of wood coals, hardwood lump charcoal, or charcoal briquettes (see page 25). Move about a quart's worth of coals to the cooking pit and arrange them in a ring (see pages 32 to 34).

FOR THE SLAW

Juice of 1 large lemon

2 tablespoons olive oil

½ teaspoon kosher salt

1 medium bunch kale, ribs removed and leaves very thinly sliced

1 small apple, cored and cut into matchsticks

¼ cup (28 g) dried cranberries

¼ cup (30 g) salted pepitas

¼ cup (25 g) grated Parmesan cheese

Ground black pepper

Lightly spray a dutch oven with oil and heat it over the coals. Melt the butter in the oven and tilt to swirl it around.

Season the chicken with a few pinches of paprika. Arrange the chicken in a single layer in the oven, skin side down. Cover and place 1½ rings of coals on the lid.

Bake over medium heat for 30 minutes. Turn all of the chicken thighs over, season with a few more pinches of paprika, and cover. Replenish the coals as needed to maintain medium heat, rotate the oven and lid for even cooking, and continue baking for 25 to 30 minutes more, until the chicken is crisp and browned all over.

While the chicken is cooking, prepare the slaw. In a large bowl, whisk together the lemon juice, oil, and salt until well blended. Add the kale and toss to coat thoroughly. Let stand for at least 15 minutes until the leaves begin to soften. Add the apple, cranberries, pepitas, and Parmesan and toss to combine.

Season the slaw with pepper to taste and serve alongside the chicken.

When it comes to complementary flavors in cooking, pork and apples are a classic pair, especially when they're cooked low and slow to draw out all the sweet and savory juices. After a couple of hours in a tangy apple cider bath, the pork turns so mouthwateringly tender that you'll need a spoon to scoop it out with the sauce. I like to use medium sweet to sweet-tart Honeycrisp, Golden Delicious, or Pink Lady (Cripps Pink) apples in this recipe, but any variety will work.

DUTCH OVEN CIDER-BRAISED PORK SHOULDER WITH APPLE AND POLENTA

MAKES 4 SERVINGS

Olive oil spray

2½ pounds/1 kg boneless pork shoulder, cut into 4 equal pieces

Kosher salt and ground black pepper

2 medium yellow onions, cut into ½-inch (1-cm) wedges

1 cup (240 ml) apple cider

3 sprigs thyme, plus more for garnishing

2 medium apples, cored and cut into ½-inch (1-cm) wedges

1 teaspoon Dijon mustard

2 tablespoons butter

1 (18-ounce/510 g) tube prepared polenta, cut into chunks

1 cup milk

Prepare a mound of wood coals, hardwood lump charcoal, or charcoal briquettes (see page 25). Move about a quart's worth of coals to the cooking pit and arrange them in a full spread (see page 32).

Lightly spray a dutch oven with oil and heat it over the coals. Season the pork shoulder generously with salt and pepper.

Sear the pork shoulder in the oven for about 3 minutes on each side, until a golden brown crust forms. Move the oven off the coals and arrange the coals in a ring (see pages 32 to 34). Set the oven on the coals and add the onions, cider, and thyme. Stir to combine all of the ingredients, then cover and place 1½ rings of coals on the lid.

Bake over medium heat for about 2 hours, until the pork shoulder is so tender that it falls apart easily. Replenish the coals as needed to maintain medium heat and rotate the oven and lid every 30 minutes for even cooking.

When done, transfer the pork shoulder and onions to a serving dish. Move all of the coals underneath the oven and bring the liquid to a rapid simmer. Add the apples and mustard and cook until the apples are just tender and the liquid reduces slightly into a thick sauce, about 5 minutes.

Meanwhile, heat a small saucepan over medium-high heat. Melt the butter and add the polenta and milk. Mash and stir the polenta into the milk until it turns creamy and soft, about 5 minutes.

To serve, spoon the polenta onto a plate, top with pork, onions, and apples, and drizzle with sauce. Garnish with a sprinkle of chopped fresh thyme leaves.

✧ USE IT UP ✧

Put your last few sprigs of thyme toward another dish in camp—like Savory Pancakes with Scallions, Mushrooms, and Goat Cheese (page 51), Bacon-Wrapped Trout Stuffed with Herbs (page 103), or Grilled Watermelon with Gorgonzola and Pistachio Crumbles (page 133).

FOR THE RIBS

2 tablespoons packed brown sugar

2 tablespoons smoked paprika

1 tablespoon kosher salt

1 tablespoon ground black pepper

1 tablespoon garlic powder

1 teaspoon ground cayenne pepper

¼ cup Dijon mustard

3½ to 4 pounds (1.5 to 1.8 kg) baby back pork ribs, silver skin removed, rack cut into 4 equal sections (see Note)

Note: Baby back pork ribs are also called pork loin back ribs.

FOR THE BRAISE

Olive oil spray

2 large bell peppers, cored and sliced

1 large yellow onion, sliced

1 cup (240 ml) beer

2 tablespoons cider vinegar

If you like fall-off-the-bone, melt-in-your-mouth ribs with a bit of heat to them, this recipe deserves a turn in your regular rotation in camp. It's got two great things going for it: a simple rub of savory spices and an easy pour of your favorite beer. As for what kind of beer, well, I'll leave that up to you (and your cooler supply), but I'm partial to dark ales for the distinct roasted flavor they bring to the dish. Start this recipe as soon as you return from your midday hike, let it simmer for a couple of hours, then clink a few bottles and toast to a day well spent.

DUTCH OVEN BEER-BRAISED BABY BACK RIBS

MAKES 4 SERVINGS

At Home

To make the dry rub for the ribs, combine the sugar, paprika, salt, pepper, garlic powder, and cayenne pepper in a small bowl.

Spread the mustard evenly on both sides of the ribs, followed by a generous coating of the dry rub. Don't be afraid to use all of the rub; these ribs can take it. Transfer the ribs to a resealable plastic bag, squeeze out the excess air, and chill for at least 1 hour and up to 24 hours.

In Camp

Prepare a mound of wood coals, hardwood lump charcoal, or charcoal briquettes (see page 25). Move about a quart's worth of coals to the cooking pit and arrange them in a ring (see pages 32 to 34).

To make the braise, lightly spray a dutch oven with oil and heat it over the coals. Scatter the bell peppers and onion in the oven and arrange the ribs on top in a single layer. Pour in the beer and vinegar, cover, and place 1½ rings of coals on the lid.

Bake over medium heat for about 2 hours, until the ribs are caramelized, the ends of the bones protrude, and a fork easily penetrates the meat. Replenish the coals as needed to maintain medium heat and rotate the oven and lid every 30 minutes for even cooking.

If you like your ribs wet, transfer the ribs and vegetables to a serving dish when they're done and cover loosely with foil. Move all of the coals underneath the oven in a full spread (see page 32) and bring the liquid to a rapid simmer. Cook until the liquid reduces slightly into a thick sauce.

Serve the ribs with a few spoonfuls of sauce on top and a side of the braised vegetables.

187 CAMP FEASTS

SIPS & SWEETS

Cocktails are stirred and desserts are doled out. Sticky spoons and forks drip with sweet sustenance. In just a few seconds, they're licked clean. Crumpled napkins sit on empty plates as the coals burn out, the sky turns a deeper black, and the stars glow brighter. Conversations quiet into comfortable silence. You feel your body aligning itself with the rhythm of the earth, and in that moment, life is complete.

Mimosa is why long, lazy mornings exist. Sangria is why long, lazy afternoons exist. Put them together and you might as well park yourself in that hammock for the rest of the day. What I like most about this recipe is that it's more of a loose guideline, open to endless variations, and hard to mess up. You can mix and match your favorite fruits, juices, and liqueurs to create a signature cocktail that's probably way too easy of a pour (or "highly drinkable," as they say in the booze world). Better make a double batch for brunch!

MIMOSA SANGRIA

MAKES 8 TO 10 SERVINGS

3 cups (700 ml) fruit juice

3 cups (750 g) fresh fruits
(sliced or diced, if necessary)

½ cup (120 ml) fruity liqueur
(such as Cointreau, Grand
Marnier, or Chambord)

1 (750 ml) bottle dry
sparkling wine, chilled

Combine the juice, fruit, and liqueur in a large jar (or pitcher, if serving from one) and let the flavors intermingle for at least 1 hour. If you have space in your cooler, keep the mixture chilled until ready to use.

Add the sparkling wine to the jar (or pitcher) and serve immediately. Alternatively, you can fill individual glasses about one-third full with the juice mixture and top with sparkling wine.

Note: In the recipe pictured, I used a blend of orange and pineapple juices, sliced strawberries and whole blueberries, Cointreau, and Prosecco.

A classic margarita is an incredibly simple beverage to concoct: just tequila, triple sec, and lime juice. But when you want to keep it even simpler in the backcountry, limeade is a clever cheat that almost makes it taste like the real thing. Ratios for margaritas can vary but here's an easy one to remember in camp: 3 parts limeade, 2 parts tequila, and 1 part triple sec.

3-2-1 MARGARITA

MAKES 1 SERVING

3 parts limeade
2 parts silver tequila
1 part triple sec
Jalapeño pepper, thinly sliced (optional)

Combine the limeade, tequila, and triple sec in a glass and top off with ice. If you like your margarita with some heat, stir in a few slices of jalapeño before serving.

Margaritas (right) may be the most well known of Mexico's cocktails on this side of the border, but the Paloma (left) tops the list as a traditional favorite in the country. Fizzy, invigorating, and smooth, it's exactly what you want on a hot, lazy, leisurely day by the water. You can try any brand of grapefruit soda, such as Izze, Hansen's, Blue Sky, San Pellegrino, or even Squirt or Fresca, but Jarritos is the most popular mixer, if you can find it.

PALOMA

MAKES 1 SERVING

1 part silver tequila
1 part grapefruit soda
Juice of ½ medium lime
Kosher salt

Combine the tequila, grapefruit soda, and lime juice in a glass. Add a pinch of salt, top off with ice, and serve.

MAKES 1 SERVING

1 part light lager or wheat
beer, chilled

1 part ruby red grapefruit
juice, chilled

✧ MIX IT UP ✧

Try a variety of fruit juices and nectars to craft your own signature shandy, such as orange juice, pomegranate juice, mango nectar, pear nectar, apple cider, lemonade, or the Hawaiian blend of POG (passion fruit, orange, guava).

English speakers know this drink as a shandy, but around the world it goes by a number of other monikers: panaché (France), clara (Spain), radler (Germany), and Sneeuwwitje ("Snow White" in Holland). Whatever you call it, there's no arguing that this refreshing beer cocktail is easy drinkin'. Though a few commercial breweries have packaged their own versions of shandies, it's a simple concoction to make in camp: just combine beer and juice. It's equally good for improving a beer you're not keen on, or enhancing a beer you already enjoy.

RUBY RED GRAPEFRUIT SHANDY

Pour the beer into a glass, then top with the juice. (Pictured left.)

MAKES 4 SERVINGS

Handful of fresh basil leaves

2 medium peaches, pitted
and thinly sliced

2 (12-ounce/350 ml) bottles
summer ale, chilled

1 cup (240 ml) ginger beer,
chilled

1 cup (240 ml) peach
nectar, chilled

✧ MIX IT UP ✧

If you're not traveling far, you can use sliced frozen peaches in place of fresh peaches to keep the sangria colder longer.

When you can't make up your mind between beer and sangria for happy hour, try a beer sangria—the happy-go-lucky, sun-kissed love child of two very respectable beverages. It's fresh, fruity, and fizzy, and makes the most of seasonal summer ales that show up for those few glorious months. Look for a light, bright, and crisp ale with notes of citrus or stone fruits to balance the spicy ginger beer and fresh ripe peaches.

SUMMER ALE SANGRIA WITH GINGER AND PEACH

In a stockpot, muddle the basil and half the peaches. Add the remaining peaches and the ale, ginger beer, and peach nectar and stir to combine. Serve immediately. (Pictured right.)

I like a good old-fashioned lemonade, but I love a good old-fashioned lemonade spiked with a shot of honey bourbon (such as Wild Turkey American Honey or Jim Beam Honey). The sweetness of the bourbon goes down smooth and adds just the right amount of booze to the kind of beverage you want to slowly swill all day by the lake. (Hey, nothing wrong with that.)

HONEY BOURBON LEMONADE

MAKES 6 TO 8 SERVINGS

5 cups (12 dL) water, divided

1 cup (100 g) sugar

1 cup (240 ml) freshly squeezed lemon juice

1 cup (240 ml) honey bourbon

1 large lemon, thinly sliced

At Home

Combine 2 cups (475 ml) of the water and the sugar in a small saucepan over medium heat. Stir until the sugar is dissolved, then remove from the heat and let the simple syrup cool to room temperature.

Pour the syrup, lemon juice, bourbon, and remaining 3 cups (725 ml) water into a half-gallon container. Depending on the acidity of your lemons, adjust for taste and add more sugar, lemon juice, or water as needed. Chill for up to 1 week.

In Camp

Serve the honey bourbon lemonade over ice and garnish with lemon slices.

LEMONADE LOVE

A good lemonade starts with the above recipe of simple syrup, lemon juice, and water. Make it even better with one of the flavor variations below.

For Herbal Lemonade: Steep a few sprigs of thyme, rosemary, mint, or basil in the simple syrup over low heat for about 30 minutes. Discard the herbs and combine the infused syrup with lemon juice and water as directed above.

For Strawberry Lemonade: Add 1 cup strawberry puree to the lemonade. Or take it a step further and use a basil-infused syrup for Strawberry-Basil Lemonade.

For Pink Lemonade: Add 2 tablespoons grenadine to the lemonade.

For Spa Lemonade: Use a mint-infused syrup and steep sliced cucumbers in the lemonade for at least 2 hours (and no more than 2 days) before serving.

For Arnold Palmer: Replace the water with strong brewed green, black, or white tea.

For Limeade: Replace the lemon juice with freshly squeezed lime juice.

Iced tea cocktails like this one are a modern spin on mixed drinks that let both beverages shine. The whiskey here (I like to use Tennessee whiskey) adds just enough bite to counter the sweetness of the Southern-style tea. But be warned: It goes down way too easily.

WHISKEY-SPIKED SWEET TEA

MAKES 6 TO 8 SERVINGS

7 cups (17 dL) water

1 cup (100 g) sugar

3 family-size black iced tea bags

1 cup (240 g) whiskey

1 large lemon, thinly sliced

Note: Lipton and Luzianne are the standard supermarket brands formulated for iced tea brewing. These are not cold brew bags, but rather tea bags that still require hot water. They're labeled as "iced tea bags" because the tea won't turn cloudy when refrigerated. You can also use your favorite black tea in this recipe; simply replace the 3 family-size tea bags with 6 regular-size tea bags.

At Home

Bring the water to a boil in a large kettle. Remove the kettle from the heat and add the sugar and tea bags. Steep for about 5 minutes, stirring occasionally, until the sugar is dissolved.

Remove the tea bags, squeeze the liquid out, and discard. Let cool, then transfer the sweet tea to a half-gallon container. Stir in the whiskey and chill for up to 3 days.

In Camp

Serve the spiked sweet tea over ice and garnish with lemon slices.

MAKE-YOUR-OWN
CAMP COFFEE KIT

If you're serious about your cup of joe in the morning and instant coffee just isn't cutting it, consider making your own camp coffee kit. By storing all of your backcountry barista tools in one place, like a pouch or plastic bag, you can have a smoother and easier start to the day when your brain feels like a blur. Below are two of my favorite no-fuss brewing systems for camping.

For 1 or 2 people:

- ✕ An **AeroPress Coffee and Espresso Maker**. The compact brewing system can make a mug of coffee in less than a minute, and it rinses clean in a snap. Simply add your coffee grinds, fill with hot water, and press the plunger for 20 seconds.

- ✕ A small bag of your favorite **coffee beans**. If you're only making coffee for yourself and/or your partner, treat yourself to whole beans and make a fresh grind every morning.

- ✕ A **hand coffee grinder** for grinding beans in camp. To save space, look for a coffee grinder that's specially designed to nest inside the AeroPress.

- ✕ An **insulated mug**. Forget enamelware mugs, which are charming but impractical for coffee. Pack a double-wall insulated mug, preferably with a lid.

For 4 or more people:

- ✕ A **GSI Outdoors Collapsible Java Drip**. This lightweight silicone drip coffeemaker fits over any wide-mouth bottle and makes pour-over style coffee—just add grinds and hot water. When done, it collapses into a disk for easy storage.

- ✕ A **vacuum-insulated bottle or carafe** for keeping the coffee hot while your campmates trudge to the kitchen.

- ✕ A pack of **#4 coffee filters**.

- ✕ A bag of **freshly ground coffee beans**. Store them in a dry, cool place, preferably in an airtight container, to maintain freshness.

- ✕ An **insulated mug** for each person.

It may not be the most authentic chai, but the ease of having a jar of homemade chai concentrate on hand for spicy mugs of tea in camp cannot be beat. The sweetened condensed milk slips some comfort into warm tea that's most welcome on a chilly morning when you don't even want to get out of your sleeping bag, much less your tent. Mix it with a robust, strong-brewed black tea, such as Assam, English breakfast, or Earl Grey, for a classic chai. If you want to mix it up, try a lighter tea like Darjeeling.

CAMP CHAI

MAKES UP TO 14 SERVINGS

FOR THE CHAI CONCENTRATE

1 (14-ounce/415-ml) can sweetened condensed milk

1 teaspoon ground cardamom

1 teaspoon ground ginger

½ teaspoon ground cinnamon

½ teaspoon ground cloves

FOR THE CHAI

Black tea bag

Hot water

At Home
To make the chai concentrate, combine all of the ingredients in a small bowl. Transfer to a lidded container and chill for up to 3 weeks.

In Camp
Steep the tea bag in a mug of hot water for 3 to 5 minutes. Stir in a few spoonfuls of chai concentrate to taste.

 **MIX IT UP**

Cardamom, ginger, cinnamon, and cloves are the core ingredients of any good chai, but you can customize the spice mix to your liking—try star anise, fennel, allspice, coriander, or even black pepper if you're feeling adventurous.

Those little packets of hot cocoa mix—you know, the ones with the dehydrated mini marshmallows in them—have a certain nostalgia that I sometimes can't resist. Chalk it up to years of camping and sipping mugfuls by a fire while trading stories about adventures and reminiscing on life. I think I like the memories associated with them more than I actually like the cocoa itself, though. So I set forth to make my own mix—one that includes real bits of chocolate and not just the dry powdery stuff. The combination of chocolate chips, cocoa powder, sugar, and a touch of dry milk powder (which you're free to omit if you always have milk on hand) makes a creamy, luscious mug of hot chocolate with deep flavor.

HOMEMADE HOT CHOCOLATE MIX

MAKES 14 TO 18 SERVINGS

1 cup (170 g) bittersweet chocolate chips, very finely chopped (at least 60% cacao)

1 cup (85 g) unsweetened cocoa powder

1 cup (100 g) sugar

½ cup (21 g) dry milk powder

½ teaspoon kosher salt

Combine all of the ingredients in a small bowl. Transfer to an airtight container and store in a dry, cool place for up to 3 months.

Classic Hot Chocolate

MAKES 1 SERVING

1 cup (240 ml) water or milk

3 to 4 tablespoons Homemade Hot Chocolate Mix (above)

Heat the water in a small saucepan over medium heat until steamy. Add the hot chocolate mix and stir until all of the ingredients are dissolved and well blended.

Mexican Hot Chocolate

MAKES 1 SERVING

1 cup (240 ml) water or milk

3 to 4 tablespoons Homemade Hot Chocolate Mix (above)

⅛ teaspoon ground cinnamon

Pinch of ground cayenne pepper

Heat the water in a small saucepan over medium heat until steamy. Add the hot chocolate mix, cinnamon, and cayenne and stir until all of the ingredients are dissolved and well blended.

This cocktail is near and dear to my heart because it's one that my friends and I have made hundreds of times on camping trips, cabin trips, and any mountain getaway where there's snow involved. More than a decade of Snuggler-fueled shenanigans have happened in at least six states and two countries! We only make this when we all get together on such a trip (which, sadly, is only once or twice a year these days with everybody scattered between both coasts), so it truly feels like a special occasion when someone breaks out the bottle of peppermint schnapps and little packets of cocoa. The cozy cocktail tastes like a warm, tingly, melty Peppermint Pattie in a cup. You can use any hot cocoa or hot chocolate in this recipe, but my Homemade Hot Chocolate Mix (opposite page) is especially heavenly with it.

SNUGGLERS

MAKES 1 SERVING

1 part peppermint schnapps

6 parts Classic Hot Chocolate (opposite page)

Stir the schnapps into a mug of hot chocolate until well combined.

 **MIX IT UP**

Another variation I like to make is what I call Smugglers—a mix of Mexican Hot Chocolate (opposite page) and peppermint schnapps, sometimes with a splash of cognac.

Mulled wine is one of those things where everyone has his or her own way of making it, and usually with a secret ingredient, kind of like barbecue sauce or the family pot roast. So, here's my secret ingredient: maple syrup. In the past, I'd always used sugar to sweeten the brew (because steeping brings out the sour tannic flavor in wine), but I found that maple syrup adds a deep, smooth sweetness that takes the mulled wine to another level. It pairs especially well with wines that have hints of dark fruit, like plum, currant, and blackberry. Go with a syrup on the darker side of the spectrum, such as Grade A: Dark Color Robust Flavor for its strong, almost brown sugar–like flavor.

CITRUS AND MAPLE MULLED WINE

MAKES 8 SERVINGS

2 (750 ml) bottles red wine

½ cup (120 ml) maple syrup

1 teaspoon coriander seeds

2 (3-inch/8-cm) cinnamon sticks

12 allspice berries

2 star anise

1 bay leaf

2 medium oranges, halved crosswise

½ cup (120 ml) brandy

Add the wine, maple syrup, and all of the spices to a stockpot over medium heat. Juice the oranges into the stockpot and add the rinds. Bring to a simmer, reduce the heat to low, and steep for at least 30 minutes to let the flavors develop. Stir in the brandy before serving and ladle into mugs, avoiding the orange rinds and spices.

WAKE UP THOSE SPICES

To bring out even deeper flavor in your spices, toast them in the stockpot over medium-high heat before adding the other ingredients.

Warm and fragrant, this mulled cider sings with heady spices (and a hint of booze) without overwhelming the delicate apple aroma. It's more than just swirling in a few cinnamon sticks or tossing in a bag of generic "mulling spices." Having the right blend of spice helps balance and enhance the natural acidity and sweetness in the apples, and if you start with great cider, you'll end up with great mulled cider. Look for one that's deep in color and cloudy with good body.

VANILLA AND BOURBON MULLED CIDER

MAKES 4 SERVINGS

1 quart (1 L) apple cider

2 (3-inch/8-cm) cinnamon sticks

4 cardamom pods, bruised with the side of a knife

4 cloves

¼ teaspoon coriander seeds

½ vanilla bean, split

½ cup (120 ml) bourbon

Add the cider and all of the spices to a small saucepan over medium heat. Bring to a simmer, reduce the heat to low, and steep for at least 30 minutes to let the flavors develop. Stir in the bourbon before serving and ladle into mugs, avoiding the spices.

A camping cookbook just isn't complete without s'mores! But you don't need a recipe to tell you how to toast a marshmallow. Rather, think of these "recipes" as inspiration for your next campfire concoction when you want to jazz up the usual marshmallow, chocolate, and graham cracker stack.

CAMPFIRE S'MORES, 6 WAYS

STRAWBERRY S'MORES

Toasted marshmallows

Strawberries (fresh or warmed over the fire)

Dark chocolate

Graham crackers

PEANUT BUTTER AND BANANA S'MORES

Toasted marshmallows

Sliced bananas

Reese's Peanut Butter Cups

Chocolate graham crackers

CHOCOLATE CHIP COOKIE S'MORES

Toasted marshmallows

Milk chocolate

Soft-baked chocolate chip cookies

NUTELLA AND SALTED CARAMEL S'MORES

Toasted marshmallows

Nutella

Salted caramel chocolate

Graham crackers

ALMOND BUTTER AND JELLY S'MORES

Toasted marshmallows

Raspberry jelly

Almond butter

Dark chocolate with almonds

Graham crackers

NUTTY CARAMEL S'MORES

Toasted marshmallows

Crunchy peanut butter

Caramel chocolate

Chocolate graham crackers

SOME MORE HISTORY

The history of the s'more is somewhat vague, but the first recipe for "Some Mores" was published in 1927 in a handbook called *Tramping and Trailing with the Girl Scouts*. Though the recipe was credited to a woman named Loretta Scott Crew, sources are conflicted on whether she actually invented the sticky snack or was merely the first to be formally credited for it. The original recipe instructs Girl Scouts to "Toast two marshmallows over the coals to a crisp gooey state and then put them inside a graham cracker and chocolate bar sandwich. . . . Though it tastes like 'some more,' one is really enough." As for when "some more" became "s'more," the contracted term came a decade later in various publications and has stuck ever since.

Everyone has his own idea of the perfect s'more. Should the chocolate be melted or not? Should the marshmallow be well charred or just golden brown? While there's no right or wrong when it comes to making the classic treat, I've toasted (and burned) many a s'more in my life, so here are a few things I've learned along the way.

S'MORES TIPS & TRICKS

You don't have to toast a marshmallow on a stick.
In fact, you don't need skewers at all. Simply assemble your s'more in the center of a sheet of heavy-duty foil, wrap it up tightly, and place it on the grill grate or near the coals for a few minutes. Use tongs to retrieve your foil pack. The marshmallow won't have a golden crust, but it'll be perfectly gooey, along with the chocolate and other ingredients.

A toasted marshmallow doesn't actually melt the chocolate.
The residual heat from a hot-off-the-flame marshmallow might make the top of the chocolate glisten, but it certainly won't melt it into an oozing cascade. Instead, melt your ingredients separately. Place a square of chocolate on a graham cracker, and set it over indirect heat on the grill grate. Pull it off once the chocolate has melted sufficiently, and top with a toasted marshmallow.

It's easy to make s'mores for a crowd.
To melt several s'mores at the same time (or if you have quite the raging fire going), place a cast-iron pan on the grate and arrange your chocolate-laden graham crackers in the pan. Transfer them to plates with a spatula once melted. The pan method also helps prevent your crackers from scorching or falling through the grate. Campers will want to toast their own marshmallows, of course!

You don't need a campfire to make s'mores.
If you have a portable grill with a lid, you can make s'mores without making a fire. Stack a graham cracker, chocolate, and marshmallow on the grate, leave the whole thing under the lid for a few minutes, and the ingredients will melt beautifully.

You can let your imagination run wild.
If you've never ventured outside of graham cracker/milk chocolate/marshmallow territory, you are in for a treat.

Step up your s'more game with different kinds of crackers and cookies, like flavored graham crackers (cinnamon or chocolate), oatmeal cookies, vanilla wafers, gingersnaps, or stroopwafel. Even pound cake, brownies, Pop-Tarts, or Rice Krispies treats can serve as tasty bases!

Explore different types of chocolate, like white, dark, and extra dark chocolate, or artisanal flavors like salted caramel, chile orange, and mint chocolate.

Experiment with your favorite jams, jellies, or nut butters, as well as caramel sauce, chocolate syrup, or fresh berries.

These melty, mouthwatering treats are a camping tradition for my crew. When the fire is starting to wane and we're yearning for a midnight snack, we put a few of these foil packs on the glowing hot embers. The bananas turn so creamy that it's almost like eating a chocolaty peanut butter and banana soufflé. They're also completely customizable and our banana boats differ slightly each time, depending on what we remember to buy or pack. To start your own tradition, create a "build your own" banana boat bar and let your friends concoct their own campfire dessert.

COAL-BAKED BANANA BOATS

MAKES 4 SERVINGS

4 medium bananas
½ cup (135 g) peanut butter
½ cup (45 g) chocolate chips
½ cup (57 g) chopped pecans

Prepare a bed of glowing hot coals in a fire pit.

With the peels still on, split each banana in half, stopping just before you slice through to the bottom. Fill each banana "boat" with equal portions of the peanut butter, chocolate chips, and pecans. Wrap each banana boat tightly with aluminum foil and place the packets directly on top of the hot coals. Cook for about 10 minutes, until the bananas are soft and the chocolate chips are melted.

 ✧ MIX IT UP ✧

These banana boats are good with just about anything—try topping them with walnuts, marshmallows, almond butter, peanut butter chips, caramel sauce, or crushed graham crackers (you know, the ones sitting in the bottom of the box that nobody wants for a s'more).

2 tablespoons honey

2 teaspoons ground cinnamon

1 cup (227 g) crème fraîche

4 pears, halved and cored

Note: I like to use Bartlett pears for this recipe, but any variety will work.

These pears are light and silky and pair nicely with a glass of rosé or white wine, which is always a good way to end the day.

GRILLED PEARS WITH HONEY-CINNAMON CRÈME FRAÎCHE

Prepare a grill over medium-high heat.

Meanwhile, stir the honey and cinnamon into the crème fraîche (right in the container for easy cleanup) until well combined.

Place the pears on the grill and cook for 3 to 5 minutes, turning once, until the pears are softened with good grill marks.

Serve each pear with a dollop of the sweetened crème fraîche.

2 tablespoons butter

2 tablespoons packed brown sugar

4 medium figs, halved lengthwise

2 medium peaches, pitted and sliced

If your sweet tooth is aching after dinner but you don't feel like making a production out of dessert, these caramelized figs and peaches will satisfy on both counts. Just a few minutes in a browned butter glaze brings out their richness without overpowering their fresh flavor. Serve them with a slice of pound cake, or spoon over yogurt for a lighter option.

SWEET CARAMELIZED FIGS AND PEACHES

In a small saucepan over medium heat, melt the butter. Add the sugar and stir until the mixture turns frothy and golden brown, about 2 minutes.

Add the figs and peaches and stir to coat. Cook until the fruits start to soften and release their juices, about 3 minutes, stirring occasionally.

Divide the fruit among serving plates, spooning the glaze over the fruits.

3 cups (360 g) Multipurpose Baking Mix (page 44)

2 cups (475 ml) buttermilk

Olive oil spray

1½ pounds (680 g) strawberries, hulled and halved

2 stalks rhubarb, sliced

½ cup (50 g) sugar

½ cup (113 g) butter, cut into small pieces

 MIX IT UP

Use any combination of fruits in this recipe, or just use your favorite one. Generally, I aim for 1½ to 2 pounds (680 to 900 g) of fruit in a cobbler.

QUICKEN YOUR CLEANUP

No matter how much you love dutch oven cobblers, there's no denying they can be sticky, messy, and hard to clean—especially at night when the last thing you want to do is scrape and season your cast iron. To simplify cleanup, line the inside of the oven with a double layer of heavy-duty aluminum foil, allowing several inches of overlap to prevent the juices from seeping through the seam. You can also use disposable parchment liners or aluminum liners that are made specifically for dutch ovens. The aluminum ones resemble deep pie pans and are sized and shaped to fit inside a standard oven.

For years, I used to make the camp cobbler found in every Scout cookbook, the one with a box of cake mix and a few cans of fruit. Then I graduated to using fresh fruit . . . along with the cake mix, because by the time I decided I wanted to make cobbler in camp, we were already at the supermarket, and picking up a box was much easier than buying everything in it. There's a reason that Scout cobbler is so popular; it's super easy, super convenient, and four fewer things to think about on your shopping list. But if you make the baking mix ahead of time at home, you can have the same ease and convenience of a box—minus any questionable ingredients.

DUTCH OVEN STRAWBERRY-RHUBARB COBBLER

MAKES 6 TO 8 SERVINGS

Prepare a mound of wood coals, hardwood lump charcoal, or charcoal briquettes (see page 25).

Meanwhile, whisk together the baking mix and buttermilk in a large bowl until the batter is well blended.

Lightly spray a dutch oven with oil (or cover with a disposable liner, see "Quicken Your Cleanup," left) and add the strawberries and rhubarb. Stir in the sugar until combined. Pour the batter over the fruit and spread the pieces of butter evenly on top.

Move about a quart's worth of coals to the cooking pit and arrange them in a ring (see pages 32 to 34). Set the oven on the ring of coals, cover, and place 1½ rings of coals on the lid.

Bake over medium heat for 20 to 25 minutes, until the crust is golden brown.

HIGH-ALTITUDE BAKING TIP

If you're making a dutch baby in camp at an elevation above 3,000 feet (900 m), a quick and dirty trick for helping the pancake puff up is to use extra-large eggs or high-protein flour in the batter, or both. The science behind this is to increase the protein sources so that coagulation can occur before the structure collapses (as a result of low air pressure). For campsites at 5,000 feet (1,500 m), try adding 1 large egg plus 1 to 2 tablespoons flour to the batter. For campsites at 8,000 feet (2,400 m) or above, try adding 2 large eggs plus 2 to 4 tablespoons flour to the batter.

Remember that elevation and humidity can vary greatly on every camping trip, so you may need to experiment with varying amounts of egg and flour before you find the perfect ratio. But no worries if your dutch baby doesn't pass the puff test—it will still be delicious.

1 cup (120 g) all-purpose flour

½ cup (106 g) packed brown sugar, divided

½ teaspoon ground cinnamon, divided

6 large eggs

1 cup (240 ml) milk

Olive oil spray

¼ cup (56 g) butter

3 medium apples, cored and cut into ¼-inch (6-mm) slices

Powdered sugar

✧ MIX IT UP ✧

Try this recipe with pears, or half apples and half pears. If it's summertime and you want to take advantage of seasonal berries (imagine how beautiful it would be if you could forage wild blackberries near camp?), bake the dutch baby with any combination of berries and scatter a handful of fresh berries on top before serving.

A dutch baby is one of those dishes that can go from breakfast to dessert and back to breakfast again. It's basically an eggy pancake—or a marriage of a pancake and a popover, if you will. Though it's typically served for breakfast, a dutch baby makes a sweetly satisfying dessert when topped with lots of luscious fresh fruit and warm brown sugar. (At home, try it with a scoop of ice cream!) It's sometimes called a German pancake, from which it was derived, and the term Dutch refers to the German-speaking immigrants known as the Pennsylvania Dutch.

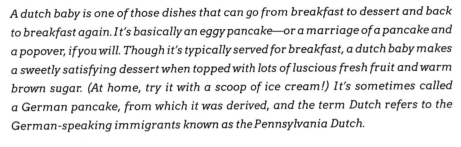

APPLELICIOUS DUTCH BABY

MAKES 6 SERVINGS

AT HOME

Combine the flour, ¼ cup (103 g) of the brown sugar, and ¼ teaspoon of the cinnamon in a resealable plastic bag and store in a dry, cool place until ready to use.

IN CAMP

Prepare a mound of wood coals, hardwood lump charcoal, or charcoal briquettes (see page 25).

Meanwhile, whisk together the eggs, milk, and flour mixture in a medium bowl until well blended.

Move about a quart's worth of coals to the cooking pit and arrange them in a ring (see pages 32 to 34). Lightly spray a dutch oven with oil and heat it over the coals. Melt the butter in the oven, then pour in the egg mixture. Spread the apples evenly over the surface and sprinkle with the remaining ¼ cup (103 g) sugar and the remaining ¼ teaspoon cinnamon. Cover and place 1½ rings of coals on the lid.

Bake over medium heat for 20 to 25 minutes, or until the pancake is puffed and golden all over. (Call the kids over to ooh and ahh at your creation once you take the oven off the heat, because the pancake will deflate shortly after the lid is removed.)

Dust the pancake with powdered sugar before serving.

RESOURCES

Here's where to find the gear seen and used throughout this book. For a continually updated list of my favorite camping and cooking gear, as well as what I pack in my pantry, visit www.thenewcampcookbook.com.

Aerobie AeroPress
www.aerobie.com/product/aeropress
Coffee and espresso maker

Backcountry
www.backcountry.com
Camping equipment and supplies

Campsuds
www.sierradawn.com
Biodegradable multipurpose soap

Coleman
www.coleman.com
Camp stoves and general
camping supplies

Dr. Bronner's
www.drbronner.com
Biodegradable pure castile liquid soap

GSI Outdoors
www.gsioutdoors.com
Outdoor cooking and camping gear

Kai USA Pure Komachi 2
www.kaiusaltd.com
Ceramic knives

Lodge Cast Iron
www.lodgemfg.com
Cast-iron dutch ovens, skillets, and
accessories

Nalgene
www.nalgene.com
Leak-proof bottles and jars

New West Knifeworks
www.newwestknifeworks.com
American-made steel knives with
leather sheaths

ORCA Coolers
www.orcacoolers.com
Roto-molded coolers

REI
www.rei.com
Outdoor recreational equipment

Stansport
www.stansport.com
Folding camp grills

Thermos
www.thermos.com
Stainless King™ vacuum
insulated bottles

TravelChair
www.travelchair.com
Camp chairs and tables

Weber
www.weber.com
Portable gas and charcoal grills

ACKNOWLEDGMENTS

As an avid camper and ardent cook, I knew this book was a dream project, a topic that stirred my soul and spurred an entire summer of camping, cooking, and exploring all over the west. The only thing that made the experience even more incredible was being able to work alongside my husband and adventure partner, Will Taylor, whose stunning photography, extensive Google mapping, tireless road tripping, and Eagle Scout wisdom was indispensable to *The New Camp Cookbook*. Thank you for igniting my love of the great outdoors, for taking the trail less traveled with me, and for sharing your passion and energy so generously with everyone who's fortunate enough to cross your path. I love you to the moon and back.

To my precious Gemma, who sprouted on the first day of spring as soon as I started writing this book. Thank you for being the happiest, calmest, and easiest baby a new mom could possibly hope for. I beam with pride when I see you outside, under the trees, on a lake, in the mountains, by a river—clearly in your element—bursting with giggles and wide-eyed wonder at the world around you: a true nature baby since your very first camping trip at two months old.

Immense love to my parents, who taught me at an early age that every gathering revolves around good food. I would not be the person I am today without their unwavering support, guidance, trust, and humor.

To my tribe, my crew, my partners-in-crime, with whom I've shared countless camp meals, campfire stories, climbing trips, waterfall hikes, hot spring soaks, river excursions, backpacking adventures, powder days, surf trips, and all-around outdoor stoke, you've enriched my life with experiences I never think can be topped . . . until we meet up for the next one! You're good people—scratch that, the *best* people. I'm beyond lucky to call you my friends.

Heaps of thanks to a most excellent troop of recipe testers and fellow outdoor lovers for their insightful feedback and enthusiastic support of this project: Erin Murtaugh, Stephen Le, Jennifer Sankary and Alan Falgout, Amanda and Jebb Stewart, Shannon and AJ Frabbiele, Christine and Will Mason, and Mikiko and David Bilbrey.

Much gratitude to my editor, Thom O'Hearn, for taking a chance on this book and letting me take the reins on its direction and content, and to the entire team at Quarto Publishing for helping *The New Camp Cookbook* come to life.

And to all the readers of the *Garden Betty* blog who inspired the idea for this book, and who continue to inspire with all the sweet notes, thoughtful comments, beautiful stories, and good vibes sent my way, thank you for following along on my journey and supporting all that *Garden Betty* stands for. You're the reason I wake up every day, excited to create, write, and share.

ABOUT THE AUTHOR

Linda Ly is the writer, photographer, and adventurer behind *Garden Betty*, an award-winning blog that celebrates slow food, slow travel, and slow living. Her love of the outdoors takes her from a modern homestead by the sea, where she grows hundreds of fruits and vegetables every season and tends a flock of backyard chickens, to forests and wildernesses all over the west, where she logs thousands of miles on the road each year and camps and cooks with family and friends. She lives in a sleepy fishing village on a little-known yet spectacular stretch of coastline in Los Angeles with her photographer husband, Will, their baby girl, Gemma, and their two pugs. Together, they enjoy surfing, snowboarding, skiing, climbing, kayaking, backpacking, and introducing their daughter to fresh mountain air, vast starry skies, and the simple pleasures of sleeping outside.

Visit her at gardenbetty.com and thenewcampcookbook.com.

ABOUT THE PHOTOGRAPHER

From as early as he can remember, Will Taylor was sneaking off with his family's various cameras and documenting the wonders of the world around him. Fast-forward to the present, and not much has changed. You'll still find Will in sunny California shooting provocative people and places for his own artistic pleasure, and for a range of clients, from Fortune 500 companies to top fashion magazines. He enjoys the travels and adventures that come with every new assignment, especially those—like the images created for *The New Camp Cookbook*—that require quests to far-off and inspiring locations. Will finds balance away from the confines of his digital darkroom by working in the garden with his wife, Linda; hiking with his venturesome baby daughter, Gemma; and partaking in all manner of extreme sports, especially his latest passion, whitewater kayaking.

For his latest exploits, visit www.instagram.com/willtaylorphotography and www.willtaylorphotography.com.

INDEX